Leaving Dirt Place

Leaving Dirt Place

Love as an Apologetic for Christianity

JONAH HADDAD

WIPF *&* STOCK · Eugene, Oregon

LEAVING DIRT PLACE
Love as an Apologetic for Christianity

Wipf & Stock
An Imprint of Wipf and Stock Publishers
199 W. 8th Ave., Suite 3
Eugene, OR 97401
www.wipfandstock.com

ISBN 13: 978-1-61097-217-8

Manufactured in the U.S.A.

To Douglas Groothuis,
my intellectual mentor
who taught me to love the Lord
with all of my mind

and to Robert Tucker,
and Jim Demolar,
whose prayer, encouragement,
and wise counsel have helped prepare
me for a life of service to Christ

Contents

Foreword

by Douglas Groothuis

WITH THE BIBLE AS their guide, Christians make the audacious claim that God is love, and that God demonstrated his love toward us by becoming Incarnate in order to reconcile us to God through the perfect life, sin-cancelling and demon-defeating death, and glorious historical resurrection of Jesus Christ, the God-Man. Therefore, the concept and reality of love vibrates at the living center of all Christian thought. This titanic claim should not be taken for granted. Neither should the concept of Christian love languish amidst clichés and intellectually superficial invocations.

While many apologetics books and articles have defended the love and power of the Christian God in relation to the miseries of this fallen world (addressing "the problem of evil"), few writers have made love itself a profound apologetic for the Christian worldview. This largely neglected task is the burden of this unique and much-needed work by Jonah Haddad. In a poetic yet philosophical approach, Haddad explains the vexed question of the very meaning of love. He then investigates which worldview best explains the objective existence of love by carefully and fairly assessing each "live hypothesis" (William James) available to answer this query.

While humans speak of love, yearn for love, give love, receive love, and have their hearts broken (and break other hearts) by the manifold betrayals of love, the very fact of love is often unexplained or (worse yet) explained away by philosophies that cannot bear its bittersweet weight. Haddad, however, does not shrink from this daunting task, but rather marshals the theological and philosophical resources required to set forth a compelling case that only the Christian vision of existence can give love its proper meaning, value, and significance—even (or especially) amidst all the tears, blood, and fears of a world "east of Eden."

Love is an inescapable mystery that has stymied many of the best of philosophers, poets, and prophets. Yet love finds its answer—philosophically, theologically, and existentially—in the person of a crucified Jew, who, two thousand years ago, manifested the greatest love of all and who gathers all other loves under his suffering arms. As George Herbert wrote in the concluding lines to "The Agonie" (1633):

> Love is that liquor sweet and most divine,
> Which my God feels as bloud; but I, as wine.

Introduction

If Love is There

SOMETHING ROTTEN HAS FOUND its way into the human heart and mind—some anger, hatred, or selfish acrimony that is set on destruction. Aggravating and irritating, it tears at the inmost places of the soul, and it gnaws on all that is good and lovely. This is the reality of the human condition: to love and to hate. This condition demands we be tattered and torn from within, to act in true and noble love toward our fellow human, and to act in vile disregard.

Hatred is all too prevalent. At times it brings the strongest of us to tears, and these tears flow harder and heavier with every augmentation of hatred's power. It is sobering. It is numbing. Hatred devastates and ruins and comes to fruition when love is forgotten. It begins with abandonment and neglect. It is bred in the wake of indifference, disregard, carelessness, selfishness, and ill-will. Ironically, it takes its form under the nurturing direction of apathy.

A loveless life is like that of an orphan abandoned by his parents and left to hardship: a little one discarded like an old worn out garment, and for what reason? The reasons may never be completely understood, but it is certain that there is a good deal of selfishness that prompts such carelessness. The one without love will lay like the orphaned child, unattended in a cold unfriendly orphanage bed, and never hear a father's gentle whisper, or feel a mother's touch.

Such reality is all too real. I have seen those who walk away from kindness, from goodness, and ultimately from love. They drop whatever is left of love and leave. They depart to pursue selfish ambitions and never look back as the beauty of love decays into a corpse. The one who walks away has lived as if he himself is all that matters. And this is where hatred begins—concern for one's self and contempt for all others. This is where indifference leads to selfishness, selfishness to hatred, and hatred to the detestation of all that is love.

The events of war often bring out such hatred. I remember reading, not too long ago, of a young Muslim woman whose life was devastated during the conflict in Bosnia at the close of the twentieth century. Soldiers entered her home and raped her, while her father and husband could do nothing to stop her torment. After these men had had their way with her and grew tired of their sport, she begged them to allow her to nurse her infant child who had been left crying on the floor. One of the soldiers struck the child, decapitating it, and threw this little one's head in the lap of its mother.[1]

Something that tears just as deep is the cruelty shown to Jewish children during the Nazi invasion of Europe. Experiments were done on these children that I cannot even mention. Words should not be expressed for these atrocities, only tears. John Weidner, a Dutch-born Frenchman who saved many Jews during the Nazi invasion of France, relates the event that prompted him to action. He remembered being at a railroad station, were a group of Jewish women and children were being deported to Eastern Europe. One woman held an infant in her arms. When the baby began to cry, an officer demanded that she make it stop. Of course, the baby was distraught and no soothing word would arrest its cries. And so the officer intervened. He forced the child from his mother's arms and smashed it against the ground, and when it did not die from the impact the officer callously crushed its head. Other soldiers only watched and laughed.[2] Weidner relates that he forever remembered the wails of that mother.

I have heard and seen far too many things that have made me question if love is there, anywhere. If we humans are to be honest with ourselves then I think we will find room to lament the lack of love in this world. If we are honest then we will question love. I have found myself asking of love, "where are you?" If love is there, then it shows itself far too infrequently. The human condition has made love compete with hatred, with indifference, and with selfishness. This has been the paradox of man. This is where we find antithesis.

---

1. This event was related by Eleonore Stump in her, "Mirror of Evil," 239.
2. Meyers and Rittner, *Courage to Care*, 59.

With this in mind I wish to pose some questions of love. How are we to define it? Does love actually exist? If love exists, does a non-theistic worldview explain such love? If atheism fails to account for love, can love be properly accounted for in pantheism, polytheism, or theism? What is the valid theistic response to love? Why is love so scarce? Can this often absent love explain the human condition? Can it shed light on humans and their relationship to the divine?

Having decided to entitle this project *Leaving Dirt Place*, I have consequently welcomed laughter, shrugs, and mild bewilderment. This title may seem a bit strange for a book on love, but greater explanation will come in the following chapters. For now, *Dirt Place* is a land where love is elusive and its origin unclear. When I began this work I had little faith in love. I was trapped in *Dirt Place* where love could not be known. Love was nothing more than a frail affection or a broken emotion. My desire was to move beyond the dry and wretched landscape where love springs up only to wither again. My desire was to move beyond such arid places so as to find a true and pure and perfect love.

1

Love: Obfuscated and Elucidated

Love Defined

E VERY FEW YEARS I am subjected to the curse of the flu like a pestilence from the abyss. Some are worse than others in their intensity and longevity, but all are uncomfortable. It was but a few years ago that I fell particularly ill. Such was the illness that my body ached with every movement, and my head was afflicted with dizziness which made it nearly impossible for me to draw myself to my feet. Between the fever and the sweating I slept uncomfortably and dreamt the most hideous dreams. Each time I closed my eyes I would find myself lost in what seemed like Dante's dark wood. There was always some peril to face: goblins, hobgoblins, and phantoms of every wicked kind. Though the illness lasted for nearly two weeks, the worst of it was at its onset. And on one of those first nights, my uneasy dreams took me to a land called *Dirt Place*. From where this ridiculous name came I do not know but *Dirt Place* was a most unusual landscape. The sun shone there but it was cold as ice. There was only dirt and sky, like in a desert but different still. Deserts are often like seas of sand stretching out to the horizon. *Dirt Place* was not like that. There were spires of sand and rock reaching like fingers to the sky, and in my dream I lay on the ground and wept for some unknown reason. The dream lasted only a short time but it was not easily forgotten. Even after my condition improved I still had a vivid image of *Dirt Place* in my mind that I have carried with me for many years.

There was something significant about *Dirt Place*. It was a land where love did not show its splendor. It was a dry and desolate place of filth; a land of discontent where everything was made frail. It was a withered place where grasslands had been burned away leaving only a pit of wretched sand and ash. *Dirt Place* was a land of weeping, where I hid with fear among the rocks. It was a spoiled land, and I think I wept so bitterly because I could not escape. In my dream I sought something. What I sought I do not know. I sensed that this land was once a place of beauty and that I was made for it but I could only lay there among the rocks, parched and angry. The dirt consumed me as I sat and watched the choking hills and flats lie lonely without hope. In the cold I watched the spires like crumbling stone tossed hard against the sky. That azure field brought comfort but even the stone like a lily unfolding kept me from escape. It was a prison, and the dry dead dirt became dear to me, for it hid me even as it seemed to lurk and watch me. Everything about *Dirt Place* was wrong. It was as if I had ungraciously lost my affiliation with a palace home. All that remained was despondency. All that re-mained was despair.

It was all a dream, and yet, like all the worst dreams it seemed so real. It reminded me of something, and now years later I know of what it resembled. Even now I look around the room or out the window and I see it: *Dirt Place*. I live in *Dirt Place* even now. I think every human being does. The good and the evil are real. *Dirt Place* had its sunshine and blue sky but it was a cage of stone and sand that seemed so corrupt and fallen. It was a hopeless, loveless place. In my dream I sensed that love was real, and yet, I could not grasp it. I could not reach out and feel it against me. Maybe that is why I wept. Even here, in the waking world love seems so elusive. Even here as in *Dirt Place*, the lack of love makes life burdensome. The love I sought in *Dirt Place* was something divine, and holy, and good. But this is not of what we humans often speak when we talk about love. I am not certain that the love I sought there can be real but still I must ask.

What is love? Much has been alleged of love thus far by scholars, romantics, artists and the like, and I often wonder how much more will be said as long as the earth continues its course and men stop to con-template all things? It was Nietzsche who said, "there is something so ambiguous and suggestive about the word love, something that speaks to memory and to hope, that even the lowest intelligence and coldest heart still feel something of the glimmer of this word."[1] Humans look for love in all the usual places. They identify it through relationships,

---

1. Nietzsche, "Mixed Opinions," 65.

through sex, through affection for various people, and through attachment to certain objects. It might be argued that every human being seeks love to some degree but what exactly is it they seek? Like the woman who sweeps her house clean in search of something lost, only to forget what it is that she is looking for, so it is with those who search for love without the slightest idea of what love is.

Those who do not believe in the existence of a God claim, even still, that love can be known. They have said that it is real and knowable. If there is anything divine in it, then its divinity is in its connection to man, the only god of the world. Yet, are those confined to earth all that is heavenly in love? Others have spoken of love's celestial origin. When Christians consider the meaning of love they will often think of it in terms of its relationship to God. The simple statement, "God is love," is spoken often as a word of encouragement and as a reminder of one of God's timeless attributes. Love of this type is thought to be an essential predication of God. In other words, to say that God is love is to say that love must flow from God as a part of his nature, or that love pours from him as a part of his essence. In fact, love is of God as of his very character. To say that "God is love" is to say that God is within his nature loving.

If love flows from God as a divine attribute then it is certain that any demonstration of love within humanity is dependent on God as its divine source. But must love flow from God? Are humans truly some god's creation, made in his image, and given moral capacities that reflect their divine origin? If God is good then one would expect to find goodness in humans. If God is just, then one would expect human beings to have a sense of justice. If God is love, then naturally humans will have a sense of love and know how to recognize this love.[2]

To those who view the Bible as true, the existence of both God and love are taken as true beliefs about ultimate reality. Yet, can the existence of love itself become a proof of a divine love giver? Is love a mere illusion to which religious people allude? Can love exist apart from the divine? As Nietzsche said, there is something ambiguous about this word. In fact, it is so encumbered by ambiguity that the truer meaning must be extracted from its many lesser connotations.

---

2. Christians believe that since the disobedience of humans brought about the fall, human goodness, justice, and love have become clouded and imperfect.

TOWARD A DEFINITION OF LOVE

There is a French proverb that says, *un amour défini est un amour fini*.[3] Yet, a proper definition of love must form the heart of any further understanding of love's existence and its relationship to both God and humans. Certainly, and most basically, love is not some corporeal object. It is not something that one might hold in the hand or toss in the air. It is not something to be hung on the wall and admired, like the work of Rembrandt or Monet. It is not a mere thing but has been seen often as some kind of intellectual or emotional attachment toward something or someone.

In his book, *The Four Loves*, C.S. Lewis identifies love within two categories. First there are the natural loves. These loves consist of what Lewis describes as liking, affection, friendship and *eros*. Operating within this first category, humans often build attachments to everything from fellow humans to animals, and from objects to ideas. These "need-loves" not only demand sentiment but appeal at a most indispensable level to the human nature.[4] We all claim such love when we speak of those things that are dear to us.

I can think of many examples of things I might claim to love. It is easy to say that I love other persons with whom I have developed close relationships. But I often claim to love certain objects of sense-perception as well. I claim to love the sound of a horse consuming a carrot or an apple. I have only heard this sound several times, and perhaps if I heard it more often I would not be so delighted by it. But strangely I find it to be an agreeable sound—a muffled wholesome sound more pleasing than a symposium of strings or a whisper in my ear. I could go on to say that I love the perfume of bread baking in an oven on any winter day when no other sensation could be lovelier. When this scent captures me it is as if something more than bread was seeping from the confines of the oven and moving about the room like an apparition. Like a siren of scent it would call me and for only the oddest of reasons I would feel as if I could only be satisfied if I were baked into the loaf itself. I could go on from here and say that I love a fire's warmth on a cold day, but only when I sit far enough away so as not to allow the radiance to sooth the chill from my body. I allow myself a taste of the flame but no more. I only sample the comfort of the flame and in doing so suspend my enjoyment of it.

3. A love defined is a love that is finished.
4. Lewis, *Four Loves*, 1–9.

I claim to love these and other things but do I really love? Can I really love such things? These are only need-loves and though the need-loves make up an important part of human thought and behavior, I shall leave these romantic and affectional aspirations to be mused over by Cupid and Aphrodite.

It is the second of the two categories that will present a more universal definition. Lewis refers to this second category of love as "gift-love." Gift-love is the sort of love that makes no demands. It is represented by a genuine altruistic concern for others. Like Lewis, Thomas Hobbes also distinguishes between need love and gift love. In the *Leviathan*, he refers to this second type of love as *charity* or *goodwill*.[5] Søren Kierkegaard states that such love is manifested in the refusal of selfishness, such as in Christ's sacrifice upon the cross.[6] Others speak of it as benevolence, or as kindness shown to fellow humans. Such love is not self-serving, but is instead, holy and pure. Containing within itself the purest of emotion, it is not characterized by emotive sentiments, nor by capricious unpredictability. Rather, it is regulated by its relationship to and passion for virtue and moral duty. In this way love is based neither solely on dry rational obligation nor on caprice.

I think it was Daudet who said that ideal love is a delusion propagated by poets. There may be some truth in this statement. Ideal love is not often seen, and is less often well defined. It is true that a variety of descriptive terms have been used of love, but can it also be true that there are many ways to define ideal love? Or could it be that there are some characteristics that differentiate ideal love from all other loves? La Rochefoucauld said that there is only one kind of love, but a thousand different copies. In a way, I think he is correct. There must be something in the most ideal love that distinguishes it from all others. It is clear that love is something good, and that it is something worthy of our time and effort to grasp and experience. Ideal love is also something not to be hoarded for ourselves. It is something to share, something to give away. This love sets itself apart from the rest by its selflessness. Such love does not take, nor does it demand anything. It exists for the help and benefit of others.

5. Hobbes, *Leviathan*, 48–60. Hobbes speaks of what he calls the "simple passions" that arise naturally within human beings as a result of desire. He distinguishes between love as kindness toward people and society, love as natural lust, love as desire to be beloved, and love as it relates to past or imagined pleasure. As an egoist, Hobbes does not defend any kind of selfless love, even though he acknowledges that it exists.

6. Kierkegaard, *Provocations*, 225.

If I were to simplify some of the above defining characteristics of love I would describe love as this: *A gift of genuine benevolence and of merciful goodwill, passionately displayed, and emanating from an altruistic concern.* Such a definition raises the meaning of love to a level beyond emotional commitment or sexual attachment, thus removing the pejorative characteristics of the lesser loves, yet in doing so it still guards the relational and emotional elements of love. Each component of this definition brings further clarity to the meaning of love, and so it is prudent to examine each of the following terms: *gift, benevolence, mercy, goodwill, passion,* and *altruism.*

Gift. The word *gift* is commonly meant to include that which is given without expectation of anything in return. When love is demonstrated as a gift it is done with little or no thought about mutual reward. It is directed completely from the gift giver to the other.

Benevolence. Benevolence is demonstrated in the desire to do good or charitable deeds, and in this way, is similar to goodwill. It is not limited to a thought or desire but is itself an intent to act in goodness.

Mercy. Mercy is important to this list because it is mercy that acts even when justice is deserved. Mercy restrains the desire to hurt or to injure and shows compassion when compassion is not merited in any way.

Goodwill. Goodwill is to be understood as an expression of moral character. Therefore, goodwill is an intentional act of carrying out kindness toward fellow human beings.

Passion. Passion here is not to be thought of as mindless, violent, maddening, lovesick irrationality. Rather, such passion is a desire for or real concern for the object of love. Love is not simply an automatic act of physics; it is something done with feeling and emotion.

Altruism. Altruism substantiates the sum of the previous terms by its unification of these under the shared idea of selflessness. The gift of benevolence or goodwill is demonstrated within a complete ignorance of the self. It might be understood as an impulse toward selflessness. In this way, goodness is established with complete disregard for the consequences that might be endured by the one who acts charitably.

Love, therefore, cannot always be seen as self-gratifying. It cannot always expect return or reward. It is not motivated by expectation of fulfillment of desire. This is not to say that there is anything wrong with the "thousand copies" of love. Love as friendship is vital to humans, for we are relational beings. We desire the camaraderie of friendship, and we thrive on the affirmations that friendship offers. Love as affection fulfills emotional needs. We humans attach ourselves to things that offer us joy and security and we claim that we love those things. Love as sexual passion plays an important role in the relationship between a man and a woman. After all, it has been said that "when there is marriage without love, there will be love without marriage."[7] Passion draws lovers together, and unites them in common desire for one another. Such love, at its best, is not easily severed. We long for love like we long for food when we are hungry or drink when we are thirsty. These thousand copies of love cannot be ignored, and the best elements of these form our definition of the ideal love which sets itself above the rest. For this love alone is worthy of bearing the name *love*.

First Challenge

THE EGOIST

Some will argue against the above definition on the premise that altruistic goodwill is not appropriate. Those who advocate ethical egoism in its various forms will object to any principle or virtue that promotes selflessness. For the self-indulgent hedonist love cannot serve others until it has served itself. In a similar way, the epicurean searches for the state of *ataraxia*, or happiness, by his submission to the pleasures. The pains of kindness, patience, commitment, and self-sacrifice interfere with his pleasure mongering and so he, the sexual vagabond, defines love by the gratification he finds in his many mistresses.[8] If love is to have any meaning for the epicurean then its meaning will be purely self gratifying.

In a similar way, objectivist philosopher Ayn Rand would reject the above definition of love by claiming that the individual must look only to his or her self-interest. She writes that as "a basic step of self-esteem, learn to treat as the mark of a cannibal any man's demand for your help."[9] In saying this Rand can only imply that one must not love. One must not give himself away in such a demeaning fashion, for to do so would be to choose "non-existence," or better said, self-defeat. It is clear that for Rand there is "only one fundamental alternative in the universe: exis-

7. French proverb.

8. Merrien, *Amour*, 35.

9. Rand, "Defense of Egoism," 78.

tence or non-existence."[10] Clearer still is the non-existence to which love lends itself. Human beings must essentially choose between existence and non-existence, based upon their propensity either toward selfishness or selflessness. If anyone is to choose existence, then that person will necessarily choose the "most selfish of all things;" this being "the independent mind that recognizes no authority higher than its own."[11]

Rand seems to echo the ideas of Rousseau who held that man's chief concern should be self-preservation. By escaping society and returning to his savage ways, man recognizes his true and only concerns: food, water, shelter, and sex. Though Rousseau claims that his ideas are not to be confused with egoism, since egoism only thrives in an established social setting, he nonetheless emphasizes self-preservation which ultimately reduces to a form of egoism. Rousseau held that the virtues of society are detrimental to humans but the basic instincts of self-preservation are enhancing to the savage man. A savage man can only care for himself, for his own existence, and for his own survival. He lives independently from others. In this way Rousseau's philosophy resembles egoism. Rousseau has separated the individual from the society, and in doing this, has removed responsibility from the individual. There is no expectation on the individual to care for others, and there is no need to live in love for others.

Nietzsche made a similar distinction by claiming that virtue will either be life-enhancing or life-negating. It is clear that Rand and Rousseau would agree with this Nietzschean thinking by placing love in the category of life-negation. Since love lacks selfishness, it lacks also the qualities necessary for life, and ultimately, for human life. Nietzsche himself was not an egoist, but for him the morality of the ubermench always rose above the morality of the herd.[12] Where the herd values those things that allow it to work together in unity as a society, the ubermench values conquest, injury, insult, and power. Such morality is a creation of the ubermench for his own life-enhancement.

---

10. Ibid., 73.

11. Ibid., 75. The authority of which Rand speaks does not entail that she is a relativist. This individual authority is still bound to the principles of objectivism, and the moral rightness of egoism, which is an absolute.

12. The ubermench or overman is a man who is superior to the herd. He rises over and above the impotent majority.

If Rand, Rousseau, and Nietzsche are correct, then love cannot be argued to be an inherent moral virtue. After all, Rand claims that neither altruistic love nor self-preservation are to be understood as instinct but as "volitional choice," because instinct is an "unerring and automatic form of knowledge" and not a simple desire.[13] For Rand, love is not natural. It is not something that a human would just do. When choice comes into play, then choice should reflect instinct. Each individual has a choice, and if the individual is to exist and flourish, then the choice is obvious: *selfishness*. After all, this is the most natural and most basic of choices. This would all make love, as it is defined above, an immoral or unnecessary feature of human thought and behavior.

Hobbes would be in agreement with Rand in that he rejected love on the grounds that it is within the law of nature to require that every individual seek self-preservation above all else.[14] Yet, love does not seek its own preservation but the preservation of others. By the standard of the egoist, any definition of love should, therefore, remain in Lewis' category of *need-loves*. The one true love should never exist, only its thousand copies. In other words, the copies of love should be practiced insomuch as they provide benefit to those demonstrating those copies. And with this in mind one must never approach love. Egoism becomes like a fallen tree within a path, set to discourage the horse and rider to return home disheartened. Egoism is the ever watchful guard that keeps love from corrupting selfishness.

Egoism certainly does offer a challenge to any form of altruistic goodwill or benevolence. However, egoism has its obvious deficiencies as well. Egoism is unable to provide a morality of resolution whenever there arises a conflict of interest between selfish individuals.[15] If all become egoists, then imagine what mighty battle would ensue. Individuals could only interact insomuch as they equally benefit from the interaction. Each individual would create his own path to success, and with it his own morality. At best egoism would benefit the few strong. At worst it would destroy humanity from within.

Egoism also creates a confusion of individual self-interests that lead to logical contradictions. This second criticism rests on what I shall

13. Rand, "Defense of Egoism," 73.

14. Hobbes, *Leviathan*, 121. Hobbes uses the term *Jus Naturale* to describe the right that every human being has for self-preservation.

15. For more on this see Rachels, *Elements*.

call the law of egoism. The law of egoism states that the most important and foundational truth is that the individual preserves and upholds his ego. With this in mind there is always confusion between egoists. For example, it is in A's self-interest to kill B, and it is in B's self-interest to prevent A from doing so. If B prevents A from killing him, then B has deprived A of A's self-interest and has, therefore, done a disservice to the law of egoism by failing to allow A to uphold his ego. Therefore, it is right for B to save himself, and wrong for B to save himself by depriving A of his duty to the law of egoism. The result is self-contradictory.

Third, the egoist must ask himself what makes any one person better or more privileged than anyone else. In the *Leviathan*, Hobbes makes the observation that the intellectual and physical differences in human beings are so slight that even the greatest differences are negligible.[16] If this is true, then the egoist has assigned greater worth to one individual over the other arbitrarily and with very little, if any, ability whatsoever to adjudicate between them. Essentially, egoism fails to offer a tenable alternative to love.

Where egoism fails, a morality of love, as defined by benevolence, mercy, and altruistic goodwill, triumphs. Since love identifies the equality of human beings and is able to serve them with impartiality, it is reasonable to maintain that such love is far superior to any self-serving and self-defeating philosophy. The universal moral appeal of love removes, by definition, the obstacles that egoism creates within its path, and human beings are sustained and served on a greater level. Common sense itself demands that love take precedence over egoism. With this in mind, love stands firm as *a gift of genuine benevolence and of merciful goodwill, passionately displayed, and emanating from an altruistic concern.*

THE RELATIVIST

Even as the established definition holds firm against the assailing egoist, who is to say such a definition is not a mere societal construct? Perhaps the definition fails to give a universal structure and meaning to love. Why must love be defined this way? Could it be that I define love this way because within my limited social sphere I know of no other way to define it? Could it be that the established definition is no more established than any other social construct that relies on its parent society?

16. Hobbes, *Leviathan*, 115.

Certainly love is not so fickle! Perhaps a glimpse of love is found in the arms of a mother as she comforts her child. Perhaps a glimpse of love is found within a hand to hold, or in a father's smile. Such a bond between parent and child has surely existed to some extent in every society and at every time. Love is not learned; it is what we humans are. I, as a child was never taught to love. I was not taught from books and lectures that love was good in the same way that I was taught that Magellan was the first to circumnavigate the globe, or that 5 times 7 equals 35. Nor was I prompted to love with promise of reward, just as children are sometimes told that if they behave well they will receive a toy or some kind of recompense in return. And yet, I searched for love and I strove to find it. Even as a child, love did not seem far off to me.

No infant is taught to hunger or thirst, nor is a child taught to make all kinds of mischief. In this same manner it must be realized that no man is taught to seek and strive for love. Indeed this desire to love and be loved is inherent within the hearts of all. Every society has an understanding of benevolence and goodwill. Every society can make sense of altruism and kindness. The fact that each might demonstrate love in slightly varying ways is no great matter. The point is that they will all have some kind of category by which to understand such things. There is a universal definition.

C.S. Lewis has illustrated the reality of universals by demonstrating that certain universals are necessary to coherent communication. Lewis illustrates this by stating that if one were to say "I feel sick," then it would hardly be appropriate for another person to say, "No; I feel quite well."[17] There is something intrinsic to physical and emotional suffering that merits sentiments of anguish and these cannot be dismissed as arbitrary opinions. The one who feels sick is justified in expressing emotionally his perceived physical condition. Yet relativism undermines the expression of sentiments by denying these sentiments of a universal context or definition by which to understand them. In the same way, when we speak of love and even express our love for something or someone, we are making a clear meaningful appeal to the existence of something objective.

Those who deny this universal meaning and make love dependent on varying moral constructs are known as moral relativists. Relativism of this kind largely developed out of the studies and research of anthropologists who noticed a lack moral uniformity when observing the vast

17. Lewis, *Abolition*, 15.

array of civilizations and their conflicting moral practices. Yet, moral relativism and its subjective understanding of love are not new to the world of ethics.

The ancient Greek thinker, Herodotus, once said that custom is king. To illustrate this claim he argued that each society will treat the deceased in a different manner. Some will bury the dead, some will burn the dead, and still others will eat the dead. In the same way, it is argued that some will live to value goodwill, and some will live to value malevolence. Yet, by claiming this, the relativist has missed an important point. In the example of the way in which a society cares for the dead, the issue at stake is an issue of practice, *not* morality. After all, each society has honored their dead, but they have simply demonstrated this honor in differing ways. Herodotus' famous claim that custom is king fails to differentiate between practice and morality. The definition of love is not a matter of institutional ritual but of intrinsic desire for that which is good.

In defense of moral relativism, some anthropologists have presented counterexamples to the normally accepted moral definitions. Some years ago, anthropologist Ruth Benedict claimed to have encountered a society that valued selfish and vengeful behavior as morally commendable. A society of this kind might very well define love as *malevolent self-interest and intrusion on the wellbeing of others.* An autonomous people may define love as such because for them this is the right, or proper, or good way to behave. In this case, so the relativist claims, the society that demonstrates "love" by what we call hatred is morally justified in doing so. According to the relativist, it would hardly be appropriate for another autonomous society to deprive the other of its malevolence. As these two opposing societies then move toward a greater degree of contact, they will likewise live in a greater degree of conflict, until one society succumbs to the pressures of the other and is raped of its autonomous moral code. Both cannot forever live according to their conflicting definitions of love.

However, on another level, whether or not Benedict's unloving society values altruism and goodwill is hardly even an issue. Just because varying societies may have varying moral standards or definitions of love does not mean there is not a universal definition that objectively applies to all people. Moreover, moral relativism collapses on itself because by claiming that there is no absolute definition of love, the relativist has made an absolute statement concerning a correct morality. Having exposed this unbecoming logical inconsistency, we may see that moral relativism is unable to offer anything more than a confusion of universally (or nearly universally) accepted ethical practices by imposing its own absolute moral principle. Given this reality, relativism adds nothing significant to love's definition, or lack thereof.

The real issue at hand is whether or not love, as defined earlier, exists. The conglomeration of letters used to communicate an idea is largely irrelevant as long as that conglomeration of letters is defined in a way that communicates something intelligible. Propositional truth is not so easily limited. Furthermore, if indeed love is not valued in certain societies, this too is largely irrelevant. Some societies may not know that the earth is spherical. They may not hold to a heliocentric model of the universe. For those, who through scientific inquiry, understand the globular structure of the earth, and who, by the same inquiry, are aware of its trajectory as it circles the sun, the truth is certain. Those who therefore deny these tested facts, whether by ignorance or flat out denial, are incorrect in their belief. Human beings recognize cosmological, astrological, ontological, and other scientific and philosophical errors, yet, too often we are unwilling to acknowledge moral errors. Given the moral confusion that has been instigated by moral relativism, I think it is reasonable to acknowledge moral realism and commit to the fact that love is a genuine object of knowledge rather than a social construct and a philosophical preference. Benevolence and altruism are morally right by definition. Just as the earth orbits the sun, love is morally right.

Human beings expect each other to behave in love. Yet, in a morally pragmatic and relativistic sense, love might be practiced by one person, and hatred by another. In this situation, relativism cannot cope, because according to such thought, he who hates will be doing right to hate he who loves. The one who loves will be doing right to love the one who hates, and accept all the hateful things that are being done to him by the one who hates. This cannot be. In truth, when he who hates goes to murder he who loves, he who loves must reject this treatment because it does not fit his morality. The problem now arises. Who is right? Should the one who loves infringe on the rights of the one who hates, by not allowing him to commit the murder? In the hateful and selfish society of which Benedict speaks, any moral dissident or reformer is immoral, for he has violated the moral norm of the society.

Consider the life of Dietrich Bonheoffer. He was put to death at the hands of the Nazi regime during the final days of the Second World War. His crime was moral dissent, for his Christian ethic would not conform to the standard of hate imposed by his society. Consider the life of Martin Luther King Jr. who opposed the unjust treatment of people of African descent in the United States. He was mistreated by society and eventually assassinated by a fellow citizen. The offense he committed was moral dissent. If the relativist is correct that virtues are only pragmatic, then anything might be permissible: love, kindness, goodness, murder, slavery, infanticide, and torture. If the relativist is correct, all of these are potentially moral, are they not?

The relativist defends pragmatic morality through his dependence on a pluralistic model of civilization. Moral relativism imposes a logically inconsistent moral absolute and demands this absolute be imposed upon all moral practices and beliefs. Yet, why should I believe this? Why should anyone believe this? Why should we accept a morally relativistic absolute simply because the relativist said so? No good argument is given beyond a few anthropological samples.

For the relativist, love and morality are dependent on the individual. When individuals are in conflict, love and morality are then mediated by the society, and when societies are in conflict the relativist must turn to something greater, something beyond mere custom. But to what, or to whom, will the relativist look?

Moral relativism will often look for its moral foundation by assuming a Darwinian model of morality, and by claiming that civilizations have evolved varying moral constructs. If humans are machines, evolved to fit their surroundings, then every moral thought and action is the result of natural processes. If love exists then it is genetic, as is hatred. If altruism exists then it is nothing more than genetic, as is selfishness. The same applies to mercy and goodwill. If moral relativism feeds on Darwinian philosophy as its nutritive source, then relativism will blossom under naturalistic suppositions. If moral relativism thrives on the belief that there is no universal concept of love, then love itself is subject to deconstruction under a Darwinian worldview.

The next chapter will examine the Darwinian attempt to explain love. As we continue on the quest for love as *a gift of genuine benevolence and of merciful goodwill, passionately displayed, and emanating from an altruistic concern*, we must honestly ask ourselves several important questions. First, in response to the scrutiny of something called psychological egoism, does such a thing as love truly exist? More specifically, can a human being genuinely display love without subconsciously seeking to realize his own selfish motives? Secondly, if love does exist, does naturalism and its materialistic metaphysic point our thirsty hearts to love's source?

Much obfuscation still surrounds love but one thing is clear; if love exists at all, it must stand up to the scrutiny of psychological egoism and it must be examined in light of Darwinian naturalism. From whence has love come? Perhaps the naturalist can tell us.

2

Toward a Genealogy of Love

Love and the Naturalist

DOES LOVE EXIST?

HAVING DEFINED LOVE AS *a gift of genuine benevolence and of merciful goodwill, passionately displayed, and emanating from an altruistic concern*, it must now be considered whether such a thing can even exist. Who among us can claim that love has withstood our self-serving and narcissistic proclivities? If such love exists then I myself have certainly failed at it. I have cast away this supreme thing: this one pure thing. I have discarded it like refuse. I have collected it as in an old tin pail only to throw it out the door of my heart like used wash water. I have buried it beneath the soil and covered it over as if to forget it ever existed. I have done all of these dreadful things as if in a dream, but have awoken to find that the horror is real. On first glance I find that love exists neither within me nor within anyone. Distant and aloof, love seems to me more an abstraction than a reality. It runs from me far more than it runs within me, and even while I chase after it I am repulsed by its procrustean attempts to mold me into something charitable and good. From moment to moment I find myself now desiring love, now resisting its allure, and all the while retaining an inherent sense that I was made to love just as a clock is made to keep time. I would like to think that I understand love's capabilities or that I know its eternal power, but I am skeptical of love. This skepticism takes me at times to the point of concluding that love does not exist.

But, who am I to say that love does not exist? Do I see love? Has the empirical eye spotted love as a watchman might spot a seagoing vessel,

16

or as a young fellow may see on the horizon the train that carries to him the girl he desires? I have heard rumors of those who have searched in what may seem to be every possible place for even a trace of love and have found but a few worn footprints or treads. I regret to admit even to myself that I have not seen love displayed wholly in humanity.

While discouraging, these elusive tendencies of love do not discount my hope that love is there. As it concerns humanity, we hope for the possibility that a drop of love may fall upon us like a small ray of light after a mighty storm. Sometimes we see love far off and run to embrace it as we would a dear friend not seen in years. We run and run but never to catch hold of love. We watch as this vapor scatters before us and weep as it forms again on a distant hill, out of reach. We have searched long and adamantly for love, like a fountain of youth or a land of gold or precious stones. We seek to love and be loved. We aspire to love in a way that is wholly unhindered.

Can love exist? Does love exist? Some will still say that they have observed love within the human race. They will say that if a glimpse of pure unhindered gentleness or kindness is displayed then it could certainly be none other than love. Could this indeed be love; and if not love then what? Is it some emotive enlightenment of the evolved man? Is it some profound and lofty emotional or cognitive state of existence that far outweighs that of the simple man, or the insane man, or the man who has come to the conclusion that bitterness, anger, and recalcitrance are more pleasurable or beneficial? All of these doubts and questions I have put forth are, in fact, the very doubts and questions that serve as the foundation for psychological egoism and its attack on love.

We have already heard the charges brought against love by the ethical egoist, but while ethical egoism claims that love *ought not* exist, psychological egoism claims that love *cannot* exist. This denial of love comes in the form of an attack on human motives. It is often claimed by psychological egoists that human love merely masquerades as altruism, when in fact it is determined by a selfish desire. Some naturalists, like Richard Dawkins, speak of a "selfish gene" which amounts to little more than an instinct of self-preservation. In fact, some will argue that human beings are incapable of acting outside their own self-interest. The argument against love proceeds as follows:

1. Human beings naturally seek their own good *exclusively*.

2. The seeking of one's own good is based on the inherent selfishness propagated by psychological egoism.

3. Love demands that people reject their natural inclinations toward their own good and seek the good of others.

4. Love, as *a gift of genuine benevolence and of merciful goodwill, passionately displayed, and emanating from an altruistic concern*, is not possible since human beings seek their own good *exclusively*.

5. Therefore, (a) love does not exist.

6. Therefore, (b) psychological egoism must replace love as a guiding principle.

Although this argument is valid, the falsity of the first premise renders it unsound. To prove that love exists one must demonstrate that human beings are in fact capable of acting benevolently without any consideration of self-gain or self-interest. It must also be understood that the altruistic concern of love, though important, is not the sole foundational principle on which love is built.

The exclusivity of selfish motivation within human beings must be called into question. Joseph Butler rose to this challenge in the seventeenth century, when he dedicated much of his work to a refutation of Hobbes. Butler reasonably concluded that Hobbes' egoistical rejection of love, if valid, must be well supported by its ability to demonstrate that humans cannot act in love. To determine whether or not a human can truly act in love Butler appealed to what he called external and internal observation.

On the level of external observation, examples abound of human beings acting in ways that appear to be truly loving toward other human beings. Consider a group of soldiers huddled in a bunker when a grenade is suddenly tossed into their vicinity. One of the soldiers immediately throws himself onto the grenade to save the others. Consider a mother who risks an operation to transplant one of her organs into her dying child, not knowing if this will be enough to save him. Consider a man, who without a moment's thought, jumps into freezing water to save a baby that has fallen. Moreover, consider a woman who finds a wallet filled with cash and does not hesitate to anonymously return it to its owner, thus forgoing any hope of reward.

These external examples would seem to be obvious proofs that love does in fact exist. However, it is the internal observations that offer a more worthy challenge to love. Internal observations deal specifically with the motivation that drives the individual to act. Furthermore, internal observations demand to know if an act of so-called love is based upon inclinations to selfishness over and above inclinations to altruistic kindness. When Butler speaks of internal observation he is presumably referring to "introspective awareness of one's own motives."[1]

In reaction to examples of unrestrained love, the psychological egoist would likely retort that in spite of their external appearance, each act of love is motivated by a hope for power, recognition, or reward. Yet, perhaps the true motivation is unknown even to the person who has acted in love. In his ethical writing, Immanuel Kant claimed often that we humans do not see our own moral judgments with proper limpidity, nor do we understand the fullness of our own intentions. What we intend as benevolence is masked behind a selfish motive that we have obscured even from ourselves.[2] If this is true the psychological egoist would then claim that every human action of apparent benevolence is in fact motivated by a self-serving desire whether one is conscious of that desire or not.

Although some claim that this is a defeater of love's existence, one might respond by showing that the burden of proof is on the psychological egoist. After all, it is nearly impossible to prove that human motivation is always inclined to selfishness. How can the hypothesis of the egoist be tested? While there are obvious benefits to showing love to fellow human beings in certain circumstances, this does not imply that every case of benevolence is selfish on some level.

Examples of love must be grouped into two categories—impulsive love and premeditated love. Examples of impulsive love would include actions that were performed as reactions without thought of consequence. Such actions are an immediate and impulsive response to suffering or injustice. Examples of premeditated love involve thoughtful and conscious decisions to act in the interest of others even at the risk of one's self. These two forms of action shall vie to demonstrate that love does indeed exist in the world.

---

1. Penelhum, *Butler*, 42.
2. See Kant, *Grounding*.

IMPULSIVE LOVE

The following are examples of love that is acted upon, in what one might call an impulsive manner. Such examples involve cases in which one has no time to think carefully through the available options. Rather, the person must respond immediately without the slightest delay.

Consider again the example of the soldier who has sacrificed his life to save his comrades. The psychological egoist might argue that there was some self-serving benefit to be gained from this action. War is brutal as any soldier will attest. The brutality of World War I is perhaps the worst any of us can imagine. Think of a young Frenchman taken from his home and his livelihood. He is called to duty and leaves his young wife and child behind. He leaves the sunshine and rolling hills of his countryside home in exchange for the smoke, the clouds of gas, and the mud of the trenches that line the border of his beloved country and the land of his enemy. Day after day he toils just to survive. Day after day he watches his comrades die. With his only friends beside him, he charges the enemy line. The machine guns awake. He returns alone. More soldiers come to replace those who fell, but there is never any hope. All is in vain. Perhaps the soldier loses all faith in his country and in the war. Perhaps he is so tired of fighting, and so burdened by all the death and suffering he sees that he chooses to end his life rather than keep fighting. Huddled in the cold one night the grenade comes in. He throws himself on it and dies. Although he saves his friends, this is no act of love, but an act of selfish gain.

This may very well be the case, yet all that might be known about the soldier's intentions has perished with him. Even if he survived, would he truly know the purity of his own intentions?

The example of the man who jumped into the freezing water to save the young child might be scrutinized by the egoist in the same way. The man had always enjoyed walking in the city park near his home. He would follow the path around the lake and watch the ducks and geese swim in search of food. He would watch the people, young and old, as they gathered for recreation. There were always children. This autumn day was cold, crisp, and quiet, and the park was more peaceful than on the usual summer days. As he walked he saw a small child slip between the rails that separated land and lake. But there were others there. In fact, many saw it happen. The child's father watched in horror. The child's mother let out a cry of terror. The man saw others there, many of whom stood closer to the freezing water's edge. Certainly they could have acted. But he did not wait to see. This was his chance. This was his moment. Since childhood he had wanted to be the hero, the one to gain recognition for bravery and for valor. Perhaps he knew that if he rescued the child he would finally be interviewed in the local newspaper and have the public's recognition. Perhaps the risk of his life was worth taking if there was the possibility of a substantial reward. Could he truly know that his desire alone was to save the child?

Other examples may be subjected to the same analysis, and every time the same question will arise: "How do you know the deed was actually performed with loving kindness or altruistic benevolence?" The answer to this question is quite simple. In these extreme cases there is no reason to think otherwise. The psychological egoist may speculate all he wants but the actions of those who demonstrate love speak for themselves. When the grenade penetrated the bunker where his comrades were huddled, the soldier had no time to think about the possible rewards or benefits. He simply responded in the most basic and natural way possible, and in doing so he exhibited love. When the child fell into the freezing water, the bystander had no time to consider the cash reward he might receive, he simply knew what he had to do. In such cases, the speculation of the egoist weighs insignificantly against either internal or external observations.

I have seen far too many cases in which people have acted in love, and when asked why, they all responded: "I don't know why? I didn't have time to think about it. I just knew what I needed to do." Will the psychological egoist make liars out of those who love? Will he make the man who loves into a selfish imposter who acts pretentiously with only his interest in mind?

PREMEDITATED LOVE

Acts of love performed impulsively and immediately run very little risk of legitimate criticism from the egoist, but what of acts of love that require careful thought and premeditation? After all, the more time is given to think through a potential act of love, the more time also is given to interpose selfish or unkind motivations. Acts of impulsive love constitute a very small minority of instances where love might be demonstrated. Surely love is more widespread than a few scarce examples. I think that most of the love demonstrated belongs to the category of premeditated love. Premeditated love forces a conscious decision for good, and for selflessness.

Consider again the mother whose child needed an organ transplant. She may have instantly known in an almost instinctual way that she would risk her life for the life of her child, yet she would be offered ample time to consider both risks and benefits to saving the child's life. In such a case, how could it be known that she had acted in true love? Is there legitimate reason for doubt in this case?

The woman who returned the lost money premeditated her decision. She may have known immediately what she must do but did she act in love? What if her display of love itself brought self-pleasure and reward? Such a selfish motive would have rendered her action loveless. Yet, again, who is to doubt she acted in true love?

There are times when decisions must be made, to love, or to go on passively with no concern. This was evident during the last great war, World War II. Now, so many years later we hear the stories of courage and hope, of bravery and goodness. We hear of those who risked their lives and the lives of their families to rescue Jews from the impending death of the Nazi camps. The hope of life that such men and women gave to the hopeless can have been the effect of none other than love. Remember the village of Niuvelande, Holland, whose entire populace collectively hid Jewish families and individuals. Each household sheltered either a single individual or family, at the risk of death to themselves. These people were not rewarded, nor were they recognized for their love. For all they knew, they would be the next to die for their actions. Yet, they demonstrated love.

Remember the old Huguenot village of Le Chambon-sur-Lignon. Led by the protestant minister, André Trocmé, the people opened their doors to hundreds of Jewish refugees. Trocmé, himself, was arrested and imprisoned for his work. Yet, even with the augmentation of the risk they were taking, the people of Le Chambon continued to love their fellow human beings. When asked why they saved so many at such a great risk, the people replied that they could not have acted differently. In a way, their decision to act was made before they had even given it a second thought. They simply acted. Above the doorway of the protestant temple in Le Chambon were the words, "Love One Another."[3] These words were not mere symbols on a post which represented some vague linguistic

3. Hallie, *Lest Innocent Blood*, 48.

conglomeration. These words were something to be lived. The people of Le Chambon understood love and they carried it out in their goodwill and altruistic concern for their neighbors.

When considering human exhibitions of love, it makes the most sense, whether one likes it or not, to conclude that love does in fact exist. Certainly love's existence can be an uncomfortable realization when one recognizes the personal loss by which it is often accompanied. To love is to sacrifice: to give of one's self with no expectation of reward. Philip Hallie notes that the value of love is the essential quality of giving one's self. "When you give somebody a thing without giving yourself, you degrade both parties by making the receiver utterly passive and by making yourself a benefactor standing there to receive thanks—and even sometimes obedience—as repayment."[4] Yet, when one gives of himself, nothing of the ego remains; all has been given. Even the personal joy and pleasure of having acted in love is subject to the act.

I think I can agree with Hallie, knowing all too well that selfless love has come to be misunderstood in my own life. I have often understood selflessness to be a lack of interference in the lives of others, when I ought to have realized that true selfless love requires me to place myself wholeheartedly and almost carelessly into the lives of those who need healing and compassion. C.S. Lewis claims that to love is to be "vulnerable."[5] If this is so, then love goes against human comfort and demands that there is something more to this virtue than can be accounted for by the egoists.

NATURALISM AND THE FINAL ATTEMPT AT LOVE

Since it is reasonable to conclude that love exists, this love must have come from somewhere. Love must depend on a lover. If there is no lover beyond man, then love derives from man alone. If there is no divine source, then the source must be of this material world. If not from a god, then love has come from a beast awakened to morality. Without God, love is dependent upon man, and so this man without God—the atheist—must account for love.

Atheism embellishes itself in naturalism in order to account for life and all its joys and pains. The ultimate concern of naturalism is nature

4. Ibid., 72.
5. Lewis, *Four Loves*, 121.

and all that is natural. Nature, of course, can be observed. It is seen; it is heard; it is tasted, touched, and sensed. In this purely natural realm there is no duality to account for the mind; there is no spirit; there is only natural stuff. There is a single substance of which the universe is made—matter.[6] Man is but a machine. But how is this machine capable of love? Furthermore, how is this machine capable of the thought necessary to perceive and demonstrate love?

Many naturalists, including Daniel Dennett, Bertrand Russell, and Richard Dawkins, believe that mind is not distinct from matter but is a function of matter. For the naturalist, no capacity of the mind, whether rational or moral requires any "transcendent power," or "extramaterial basis."[7] Therefore love is not an emotional, intellectual, or spiritual response to God or other humans. Rather, it is an effect of natural causes. There was no love, no virtue, and no reason before there was man, and so the naturalist claims that nature somehow created love, along with virtue and reason.

The naturalist claims that ethical principles emerge from human matter, but how? How can the material bring about the immaterial (consciousness, ideas, ethics)? It must be asked: what makes values? And to this it is said that humans make values. But what makes humans capable of making values? Natural process and instinct make humans capable of making values. This value then comes ultimately from the material. If the cosmos, and the matter from which it is made, is all there ever was, all there is, and all there ever will be, as Carl Sagan infamously suggested,[8] then there is no obvious explanation, philosophically or scientifically, for why rationality could arise from any mineral, plant, or meat machine. What then do naturalists say in regard to love and its origin?

Some existentialist philosophers have tried to answer this dilemma by viewing man's ethical beginnings as a moral *tabula rasa*. Jean-Paul Sartre has stated that "man exists, turns up, appears on the scene, and only afterwards, defines himself."[9] Sartre goes on to say:

> If man, as the existentialist conceives him, is indefinable, it is because at first he is nothing. Only afterwards will he be something, and he himself will have made what he will be. Thus, there is no

6. See page 177 of Torrey's *Les Philosophes*.

7. Sire, *Universe*, 73.

8. Sagan, *Cosmos*, 1.

9. Sartre, *Existentialism*, 15.

human nature, since there is no God to conceive it. Not only is man what he conceives himself to be, but he is also only what he wills himself to be after this thrust toward existence. Man is nothing else but what he makes of himself.[10]

With this being said it is possible for man to invent man. The matter is there—where it came from is of little importance—yet only later can the man as we know him exist. The nature, which is vital to all humans, must come from the matter, and so man the matter must "create" man the essence.

However, this existentialist thinking collapses in the face of the question: How is essence "created" unless creativity, which is an aspect of essence, precedes essence itself? In other words, if existence precedes essence, how then can creativity be established unless a creative nature is already in place? The creativity, from which love would then derive, must therefore be a necessary requirement for proper existence to occur. The animated organism we call man must have in place all that is required to give and receive love.

Two things are said by Sartre to be required of man. The first is choice, and the second, responsibility. Man has no choice *but to* choose to make moral decisions. Likewise, man is responsible for his choices. He carries the burden of liability for his actions whether he wishes to or not. There is no escape from these things. For the existentialist, both are essential. In fact, choice and responsibility lie at the very foundation of humanity.

The problem that Sartre and other existentialists create by placing so much value on choice and responsibility is that these two begin to look very much like an inherent human nature. In one breath humans are said to enter the world without essence, and in the next breath humans have a nature of resolution, liability, innovation, and dexterity that guides and defines their ability to define themselves.

Existentialism is unable to give an adequate naturalistic explanation of human nature, and all the more, it is unable to give a cogent reason why love exists or why it is good. In response to this, Sartre has tried to demonstrate that love is good for humanity because it is good for the individual. The individual makes decisions for himself that are reflected on humanity. Just as he is responsible for himself, so also is he responsible for humanity. If he values love, then humanity ought to

10. Ibid., 15.

value love as well. Yet, a life of consistent love is rarely as good for the individual as is a life that mingles some selfishness and hatred. After all, if one loves perfectly at all times then a certain amount of self-sacrifice is required of him, and this is not necessarily advantageous.

Though this is true, the existentialist would likely respond that since the individual is responsible for humanity as a whole, then he also must love out of concern and accountability for his fellow human. But the existentialist is yet to answer why responsibility to the larger populace ought to be valued over self-gratification. If man creates himself and finds that he is the measure of all things, then responsibility to the world means nothing. The inventor can invent a world where only he has value. The creator can create a world where only he, the individual, has worth.

Stepping outside of the realm of existentialism, there are other naturalists who attempt to demonstrate love's natural origin by appealing to the nonreligious man and his possession of moral superiority. André Comte-Sponville makes this very claim as he points to the teaching of Jesus himself, reminding us of the story of the "Good Samaritan," and claiming that Jesus himself was more impressed with the charity of a nonreligious man than with the hypocrisy of the religious elite. In the story a traveler has been accosted, beaten, and left for dead at the hands of robbers as he makes his way to Jerusalem. As the injured man lays helpless on the side of the road three other travelers pass by. The first two are religious leaders of the day. Both are theists, and both adhere strictly to their religious convictions. But these two move on with complete disregard for the injured man. It is the third man, who belongs neither to the religious leadership nor to the Jewish religious life, who stops to help.

It is the belief of Comte-Sponville that Jesus' concern was not to defend a morality that proceeded from God and his worshipers, but rather, to teach his followers that moral conduct flows most naturally from man as brute creature. The moral conduct of the brute creature must not be corrupted by religious inebriation. Thus, Comte-Sponville is confident that, religious or not, man can live a life of love not because of belief about the divine, but because of his intrinsic understanding of "la valeur d'une vie humaine."[11]

---

11. Or "the value of a human life." Comte-Sponville, L'Esprit, 65.

Comte-Sponville makes a good point by claiming that moral action does not necessitate belief in a god, however, considering the frequency with which Jesus draws a relationship between metaphysical belief and morality in the Gospels, it is impossible that Jesus was indifferent to man's spiritual state when telling these parables. Metaphysical beliefs are of utter importance here, because moral conduct is a byproduct of the way in which reality is perceived. Only when man is reduced to beast or meat machine is his conduct rendered morally neutral. In a purely natural universe morality must be based on genetic fatalism and social conditioning. A universe of this kind is one of metaphysical materialism.

METAPHYSICAL MATERIALISM
AND THE REALITY OF LOVE

St. Augustine once asked himself in his *Confessions*: "What is the object of my love?"[12] In essence he has asked: To whom or what is my love to be directed? On what is my love to be focused?" Such questions as these merit response, but before these insightful inquisitions into love's purpose can be answered, it must first be asked: "What is the objective reality of my love?" After all, how is one to love if he knows not what love is, and how is he to know what love is if he does not understand its source. Finding love's source begins with an examination of the worldviews that make an attempt to explain it. Thus far on this important subject, naturalism has contributed very little nutritive content to the digestive processes of the mind. But before naturalism is simply discarded, it must be examined in its raw materialistic form. There is no need to advance to the mystical realm of pantheism or to the supernatural sphere of theism until the world of matter has been more thoroughly examined.

At its foundation, metaphysical materialism provides a framework by which the atheist's moral position is to be understood. In considering this position one need look no further than Bertrand Russell's vivacious account of the formation of human moral conduct as springing from the process of evolutionary advancement:

> For countless ages the hot nebula whirled aimlessly through space. At length it began to take shape, the central mass threw off planets, the planets cooled, boiling seas and burning mountains heaved and tossed, from black masses of cloud hot sheets of rain

12. St. Augustine, *Confessions*, 183.

deluged the barely solid crust. And now the first germ of life grew in the depths of the ocean, and developed rapidly in the fructifying warmth into vast forest trees, huge ferns springing from the damp mold, sea monsters, breeding, fighting, devouring, and passing away. And from the monsters, as the play unfolded itself, Man was born with the power of thought, the knowledge of good and evil, and the cruel thirst for worship.[13]

All of this was accidental, and was the result of the "collocations of atoms."[14] As human beings awoke to consciousness, they created for themselves a God who was thought to be "all-powerful and all-good."[15] For the materialist this God was our creation. What tragedy it was that we humans crafted for ourselves this unneeded oppressor, always hissing words of guilt and moral shame into our tired ears. From this divine tyrant, unbearable and undeserved blame was thrust upon us.

Russell mourns this tyranny that human beings have created for themselves. He mourns the human unwillingness to repudiate the tyrant. Most of all he mourns humanity's pathetic and tragic attempt to please a God who is not there. Russell has so eloquently proclaimed that there is nothing more than atoms. There is nothing more than material. Humans are organic machines, assembled from the primordial ooze of an age long past. Thus, human beings exist for the purpose of reproducing into better human beings who might, in turn, result in something far better. For Russell and many of his peers, both then and now, this process of evolved awareness continued until morality was formed:

A strange mystery it is that Nature, omnipotent but blind, in the revolutions of her secular hurryings through the abyss of space, has brought forth at last a child, subject still to her power, but gifted with sight, with knowledge of good and evil, with the capacity of judging all the works of his unthinking Mother.[16]

Just as nature gave birth to human beings, so also, human beings gave birth to morality. Yet to what sort of morality has metaphysical materialism given birth? Life is short and the doom of the human race is impending. Humans are a mere speck in the scope of time and in the vastness of space. During this episodic and pithy duration of time

13. Russell, *Free Man*, 313.
14. Ibid., 314.
15. Ibid., 314.
16. Ibid., 314.

humans must ask themselves how they might appropriately react to one another as entities that carry the weight of moral awareness.

Russell responds, in reaction to the violent, uncongenial, and enigmatic universe, that human morality is to live in benevolence to fellow humans since we all suffer on the common path of doom and destruction. Russell exclaims, "to abandon the struggle for private happiness, to expel all eagerness of temporary desire, to burn with passion for eternal things—this is emancipation, and this is the free man's worship."[17] Here, selflessness and goodness are stressed. Here, Russell proclaims that those who are free from the bonds of belief in God can now unite under the "tie of common doom," and respond to one another in love.[18] Yet, Russell fails to explain from where love comes. He never truly acknowledges a source for the attitudes and behaviors that define love. From what source derives such desires to act? Did love, like humans, grow in the seething ponds of primordial glop and somehow attach itself like a leech to human minds? Though Russell has not explained, others have come to expound upon his sentiments.

In fact, many decades later, other materialists have risen to echo the words of Russell, and offer an explanation for the source of and reasons for love. Among these materialists is Sam Harris who remarks that, "everything about human experience suggests that love is more conducive to happiness than hate is."[19] Harris goes on to say that "while feeling love for others is surely one of the greatest sources of our own happiness, it entails a very deep concern for the happiness and suffering of those we love. Our own search for happiness, therefore, provides a rationale for self-sacrifice and self-denial."[20]

Within his materialistic framework Harris suggests that the intertwining of love and happiness is itself love's source. After all, love for others brings personal happiness, which in turn brings a desire for the happiness of others, which in turn brings love. This love perpetuates the original happiness that was experienced through love. In this way a virtuous and moral life of self-sacrifice and self-denial is made possible. This wheel of love goes around and around, each time with greater intensity. It is like laughter welling in the heart of a child who finally lets

17. Ibid., 316.
18. Ibid., 317.
19. Harris, *Letter*, 24.
20. Ibid., 24.

his giggles of merriment burst forth to the amusement of others who follow suit. The laughter carries on as each child's joy acts as a mechanism producing further joy, until all are rolling about with hilarity.

As laughter produces laughter, so also, love produces love. Yet, a word cannot define itself. Love is not itself an accurate source for love. Harris fails to offer a viable account of love's origin. At best he shows us the obvious benefits of love by stating that love seems more conducive to happiness than does hatred. Would any sane person disagree? Who, but the masochist, the sadist, or the egoists would deny the goodness of love? Who can deny love's value and magnitude? To say that love is worthwhile may be true, but why? From whence did love come? Did it simply rise up out of the ground? Did it permeate our hearts while we lay sleeping one night? Is it the result of a birth defect? Did it attempt to suffocate our survival instinct and destroy our desire to endure as selfish egotistical wretches?

In response to the questions of love, altruistic behavior, and moral and sentimental origins, Richard Dawkins attempts to probe the depths of love's foundations by launching a thorough examination of the *selfish gene*. He states that the one predominate quality of organisms that will go on to survive and reproduce is "ruthless selfishness."[21] Such selfishness on the macro scale begins on the micro scale. It begins with the gene whose sole purpose is survival. This non-sentient gene will do at least one thing: survive. It will pass itself on to the next generation at all costs. It must. Its survival depends wholly on proliferation.

To survive the gene must pass into a new vessel, and from that vessel it must pass itself again. The gene will use its carrier, whether man or woman, to seek out an appropriate mate, and thus pass to another generation. This may require rape; it may require sexual relationships with any number of partners; it may require any possible means necessary for the gene to perpetuate itself. If the gene is to survive, then its host is to survive. If its host is to survive then this host must be fit to survive. And as Charles Darwin observed so long ago, the fittest will naturally be in the best position for survival.

Robert Wright has observed that "moral sentiments are used with brutal flexibility, switched on and off in keeping with self-interest."[22] For the materialist, love is, therefore, genetically based and unreliable. The

21. Dawkins, *Selfish Gene*, 2.
22. Wright, *Moral Animal*, 13.

gene that ultimately survives is the one that gets "copies of itself into future generations in large numbers."[23] With this being said, love can never exist, because at the foundation of every human action is the selfish inclination toward self-preservation.

Both Wright and Dawkins would have to acknowledge that love does not make evolutionary sense. Yet, Dawkins does recognize that good, merciful, and altruistic behaviors do occur. But how can this be? If all behaviors are reducible to genetic selfishness then it is doubtful that goodness or altruism could ever truly exist. Furthermore, how can love be something for which human beings strive? How can we long for and practice that for which we have not evolved any genetic capacity? From where does this genetic propensity toward love derive? Like Wright, Dawkins suggests that even though true pure love is not something for which humans have a natural capacity, generosity and altruism can be taught.[24] Humans can reach beyond their genetic fatalism and learn to love. They can aspire to "upset" the selfish gene, and make a more tolerable society through the giving of mercy, goodness, and passionate selfless kindness.[25]

Of all these things alleged, Dawkins is correct only so far as he acknowledges that evolution demands selfishness, viciousness, and flat out repugnancy. He is correct that love cannot exist in a Darwinian model. Yet, his logic falsely leads him to conclude that love is possible. How can this be? Dawkins reasoning leads to the following argument:

1. Evolution has perpetuated a selfish gene which renders love naturally impossible.

2. Yet, love is a good and useful quality,

3. Therefore, humans ought to teach one another to love.

It is clear the conclusion is so detached from the first two premises that it is impossible to derive any sense from the argument. The first premise alone disqualifies the conclusion from obtaining anything meaningful. By Dawkins' reasoning, there should not even be a noetic category that allows for the comprehension of love. Furthermore, even if

23. Ibid., 56.
24. Dawkins, *Selfish Gene*, 5.
25. Ibid., 5. See also, Dawkins, "Atheists for Jesus."

humans somehow could imagine what love might be like, their genetic makeup would not allow them to act lovingly.

For example, observe the human race. Most humans do not grow much taller than about six feet. They are made of flesh, blood, and dense bone. They can be visibly seen but one cannot see through them as if they were transparent. Now suppose humans began to teach their children to grow to a height of 20 feet. Suppose that these children were taught they must become transparent like glass. Certainly this is not only impossible but foolish as well. In the same way, it is impossible to teach a child love when there is no genetic ability for the child to act in a loving way. In the world of materialism, we humans are subject to none other than the material from which we are made. Love and hatred mean nothing, for they are but a collision of material against material.

In a world where the gene reigns supreme and existence is limited to corporeal material, a nonphysical property, such as love, must be rendered meaningless. As said before, love is not seen, or touched, or sensed. Love weighs nothing, nor does it occupy space. To speak of love in physical terms is to speak utter nonsense. Yet, this language of nonsense is precisely the one spoken by metaphysical materialists who deny the non-material realities of our world while clinging stubbornly to those very realities. There is nothing material about events, numbers, rationality, meaning, concepts, propositions, or morality, and there is certainly nothing material about love. If the materialist is to speak of love, then he must throw off the material yoke to which he is bound, and allow himself access to the unseen reality around him.

This unseen non-material world of concepts is one that cannot be denied by the practitioner of materialism, for the groping reach of empirical science cannot lay hold of that to which individuals have private access. Though all human beings experience this physical world in varying degrees of ability and vigor, each one will gather from his experience a private and personal result. For example, as I gaze out my window at the city around me, the sun breaks defiantly through the wet vaporous cloak that spans the autumn sky and beams luminously on the buildings across the street. Their façade now seems to me a light gray color. As I perceive the color gray I realize that this is a sensation to which I alone have access. Though I may be mistaken in my knowledge of the actual color of the building, I am not mistaken that I perceive the color gray. In a similar way, all of my reasons, emotions, intentions, and thoughts surrounding love are inaccessible to the realm of material experimentation and observation.

Love is the result of a conscious moral choice not a programmed mechanical movement. Having removed the mind and the emotions from love, the metaphysical materialist is left with something that resembles love, but which lacks living breathing substance. All that defines love is replaced with involuntary genetic reflexes.

Even among these great proponents of atheistic ethics it has been admitted that "there is nothing approaching agreement on where we might turn for basic moral values—except, perhaps, nowhere."[26] The materialists themselves have spoken this damning pronouncement upon their own ethical system. Darwin was wrong to think that things evolve for the greater good, for there is no greater good, only a lesser one. There is only one thing, and that is the good of the gene, the individual gene. There is only one morality, and that is selfishness, abuse, and exploitation. All that matters is that "my heredity material is the most important material on earth; its survival justifies your frustration, pain, even death."[27] The needs of the society, the group, or the colony cannot matter. Even this attempt at defending love's existence in a materialistic model by injecting it into the group setting still fails, because under the veneer is the necessary reality that every act of goodwill and altruism is performed with an undertone of savage and brutal selfishness.

This poses a problem for the materialist in that human experience points to the benefit of love over hatred, to benevolence over oppression, to goodness over insult, or to altruism over obtrusion. Metaphysical materialism is unable to justify making a claim to love since the evolved human meat machine is incapable of showing love to another human being. The basic desire for self-preservation cannot lead to a desire for the preservation of others. Furthermore, even if it were beneficial to one's self to preserve another, how could such a desire share a common bond with *a gift of genuine benevolence and of merciful goodwill, passionately displayed, and emanating from an altruistic concern?*

That which is known of love should have no place within this materialistic worldview. The honest atheist is the atheist who acknowledges this and teaches others to do the same. Nietzsche was one such atheist. He was a man who saw something not yet seen by the crowds around

26. Wright, *Moral Animal*, 328.
27. Ibid., 338.

him—the need to acknowledge the death of God, and to cast off the impairing Christian moral absolute. Nietzsche proselytized for God's death and for the death of the philosophy and culture that had been linked to God, and by doing this he crafted a new moral order. Thus, human nature and values were no longer dependent on God but on human evolution.[28] Nietzsche stated that, because of the death of God, the hearts of the "philosophers and free spirits" can be filled with "gratitude, amazement, anticipation and expectation."[29] With God now removed from the context of human life and thought, Nietzsche was able to rejoice in the fact that "at last the horizons appear free to us again . . . at last our ship may venture out again" to allow that all the daring of the lover of knowledge may be permitted once more.[30]

Now, within this new morality, humans need not look to God or some abstract idea of the *Good* in order to find morality. Rather, morality can derive from within the human being. As a prophet of the death of God, Nietzsche's view of morality stemmed not from arguments made on metaphysical grounds, but on historical grounds.[31] Nietzsche made little effort to give extensive refutations of the existence of God. He did not focus on final, logical disproofs of metaphysical and epistemic problems. Rather, he examined various positive and negative implications involving ethical matters. Nietzsche attempted to observe the human condition and the way in which humans *apparently* develop their morality. His evaluation of morals was far more psychological than it was philosophical. It was an evaluation in which Nietzsche emphasized the idea that instinct ultimately leads all humans to moral understanding.

The influence of Darwin's theory of evolution is plainly seen here as Nietzsche paints a picture of the barbarian: the human who developed over time to realize a desire for strength and power. In claiming

28. The atheist who carries materialism to its logical conclusion is the truly intellectually responsible atheist. Such atheists have shed the morality of the weak, and have created the morality of the strong. Such morality was clearly seen in the 20th century with the onset of Nazism, Communism and other atheistic regimes whose existence was responsible for over 100 million deaths around the world. Human life was of no consequence. Humans would be treated only as a means to an end. In this way, not only does materialistic atheism show its ugly head, but the ethical problems of a utilitarian ethical model are also exposed.

29. Nietzsche, *Gay Science*, 448.

30. Ibid,. 488.

31. Holmes, *Fact, Value, God*, 163.

that such barbarians "threw themselves upon weaker, more moral, more peaceful races" Nietzsche justified his claim against the self-annihilating morality of the religious throng that easily succumbed to conquest.[32] His moral knowledge was, therefore, known through the raw instinct to live. All other explanations were limited to otherworldly abstractions. The need for transcendence, and ultimately for God, was therefore excluded, discredited, and finally dismissed as a "crutch for the weak."[33]

By removing God, Nietzsche was able to affirm that the "world lacks a natural, rational, or divine order, that morality is artifice and pathology, and that the will is sovereign."[34] Morality, therefore, issues from human creativity as does logic and truth.[35] For Nietzsche, God, logic, and propositions of truth, are not things that are waiting to be *discovered* by the human race, rather, these things are *produced* by the human race. For Nietzsche, truth and logic were thought to control the realities that humans structure for themselves but these things were not reality in and of themselves.[36]

In light of these considerations, one must ask then how Nietzsche is to ground his view of moral value. Just as Russell, Harris, Dawkins, and Wright have done, Nietzsche proposed that deontological moral value be eliminated through the removal of God from his ethical framework. Yet, unlike the others, Nietzsche dismissed any objective value found in love. The highest values with which Nietzsche was concerned were physiological demands for the preservation and enhancement of a certain type of life.[37] In other words, if a human being finds that violence, exploitation and selfishness promote the desired life, then these things are of moral value.

32. Nietzsche, "Beyond Good and Evil," 117.

33. Holmes, *Fact, Value, God*,162. While Nietzsche rejects knowledge of the transcendent, he does cling to at least one metaphysical principle, that being, the "will to power." The will to power is not some far removed metaphysical principle that leads humans to look to an otherworld. Rather, it is ingrained with the *Ubermenschen* and leads these noble men to life beyond the herd. For Nietzsche, otherworldly pursuits are life-negating since such pursuits distract from reality and cause humans to look to a realm that does not exist and can not be proved to exist.

34. Berkowitz, *Nietzsche: Ethics*, 26.

35. For more on Nietzsche's ethic, see *Holmes, Fact, Value, God*, 160–172.

36. Ibid., 163.

37. May, *Nietzsche's Ethics*, 9.

The need of primitive humanity was survival and procreation. If a man could not secure a mate peacefully, then he would naturally take one by force. He would defend his prize to the death if anyone challenged him. He would band together with other men to ward off attack only in his own interest. If he protected his mate, then it was for the benefit of the offspring that she would produce. Likewise, she had no attachment to him beyond her own basic need for survival. This primitive man would never lay down his life in love for another, even his own offspring. He would die not to save a life but only to protect what was his. It was not love that drove such people to care for their offspring; it was the instinct of survival.

Such an instinct could never have formed into *a gift of genuine benevolence and of merciful goodwill, passionately displayed, and emanating from an altruistic concern*. In essence, such an instinct could never have formed into love. Egoism is the only viable result of metaphysical materialism.[38] The ethic of atheism should necessarily be one of appropriation, injury, conquest, suppression, severity, obtrusion and the like.[39] This is the most natural life; this is the most noble life; and ultimately, this is the virtuous life. The noble will have "faith in oneself, pride in oneself, and a radical enmity and irony toward selfishness."[40]

For Nietzsche, the morality of Christian Europe in the nineteenth century was useful only insofar as it governed and controlled the herd in order that the *overman* or superman might create his own values and rise above his present state.[41] The usefulness of Christian love and charity amounted, therefore, to little more than a boundary to retain the masses. Even now love depreciates the impulses, instincts, and passions, of the mind.[42]

These honest and morbid conclusions about love lead to a sharp contrast between Nietzschian ethics and the ethics of his materialist associates. While Nietzsche welcomes (though perhaps reluctantly) the inevitability of nihilism as a necessary next step in the development of

38. It must be remembered that Nietzsche was not an egoist but, rather, a warped virtue theorist. However, some form of egoism seems to be the most viable result of his nihilistic ethic.

39. Nietzsche, "Beyond Good and Evil," 118.

40. Ibid., 119.

41. Copleston, *History*, 402.

42. Ibid., 405.

a higher man, other materialists attempt to cling to love, hoping that they might find some way to justify its presence in their philosophical system of belief. Wright has said that "love makes us want to further the happiness of others; it makes us give up a little so that others (the loved ones) may have a lot."[43] But this is not true. There is more to love than this—much much more. Love makes us give up everything so that the loved one may understand what once seemed unfathomable.

There is great irony in the materialistic view of man. Man was fashioned by the process of his divine but unthinking mother, the universe. Now it is this thinking moral animal that must impose its created morality upon its god. Somehow a loving humanity must love and care for its unloving creator.

Nietzsche has offered a reasonable explanation for why love ought to be done away with in light of metaphysical materialism, but he fails to give a reasonable explanation of where love came from in the first place. The objective reality of love is that it cannot come from a material cause. Metaphysical materialism not only fails to answer Augustine's question of the object of love, it fails to answer the question of the objective reality of love. For the materialist there is no objective reality in love, and therefore, there is no object of love. If God is dead, then the world and everything in it is the result of mindless material processes. For the materialist there are only two conclusions: the first is to deny love, and the second is to scorn love. Dawkins and Wright have taken the path to denial, melting love and hatred into the same reeking fondue of predetermined genetic programming. Nietzsche, on the other hand, has chosen to abhor love and treat it as an odious degrading stench in which there is nothing good, or true, or noble. In essence, the materialist has ensured that love be ruined.

He has created a dilemma that he is unable to answer, and incapable of solving. It is unreasonable to accept a naturalistic explanation for the mind, the body, and the moral conscience. The atheist has clothed himself in naturalism and metaphysical materialism with its invisible explanation of mind, virtue, reason, and love. He has claimed that only the truly wise man will see and understand his explanation of reality. His clothing was thought to be ornate, and Emperor Atheist has long paraded about, proudly displaying his naturalistic costume, when all that

43. Wright, *Moral Animal*, 341.

has ever been needed was for some brave and honest child to say, "look the emperor hasn't any clothing on."

Atheism is a transparent explanation for love which lacks any substance. The flamboyancy of naturalism's account of the mind and morality has been reduced to the rags of metaphysical materialism. If matter is all they demand, then matter is all they shall have.

Yet, so many remain mesmerized by the valiant self-surety of metaphysical materialism as it masquerades in the shallow confidence that it is still a handsome and pleasing worldview offering an answer. This worldview is the result of the work of men and women who need to know but know not where to turn. This is the work of men and women who have thought that humanity was indeed the measure of all things. This is the work of men and woman who look no farther than themselves and see nothing. Perhaps humanity disappoints. Perhaps we are not the answer to love. *Dirt Place* will not be escaped that easily.

3

The Gods of Silence

Love and the Pantheist and Polytheist

IMAGINE A GAME IN which a player is told to use all his senses, with the exception of sight, to guess which of many plates contains a certain food. The player is blindfolded and brought to a table in a dimly lit room. Before him on the table are set five dishes. His challenge is to identify a plate of roast beef. He goes to the first, and smells the contents of the plate. A pungent odor meets his nose. It is the scent of leather, sweat, and mildew. He gropes for the plate. He feels a rough oblong object. There is something like strings binding it in one place, and it is smooth on its bottom side. The player taps the object with his finger. It is hollow. He bites into the object, grimaces, and cusses aloud. Dropping the shoe, he goes to the next plate repeating his meticulous investigation. Here he finds a bowl of steam. He moves to the next and finds a plaster imitation of a roast beef dinner. He then samples the fourth dish and is again disappointed. Only after this does he finally come to the plate of roast beef. He smells it. He touches it. He tastes it. There is little doubt that he has finally identified the winning dish.

Identifying a valid philosophical position, is much like identifying food while blindfolded. On some level every belief about reality will lack certain completely verifiable proofs that, in turn, will restrict the human mind from ever approaching intellectual infallibility. There is no philosophical position, worldview, or religion immune to skepticism or doubt on an intellectual level, yet when opposing positions are laid out side by side and examined thoroughly, there should be little doubt which one (or ones) offers a better explanation and which are clearly lacking. Valid philosophical positions must cohere to reality. They must explain human nature, and present a clear insight into truth. A valid position will be logical, and a valid position will remain true while others are proved false.

Naturalism and its materialistic counterpart have already been eliminated as reasonable explanations for love's existence. For this reason it is sensible to conclude that there is a valid supernatural origin to love. But what is this origin? Is it Eastern pantheistic non-dualism? Is it polytheism? Is it theism? And if it is theism, then is it the Islamic or Judeo-Christian position that best explains love? Let us first observe pantheism.

PANTHEISM: TO LOVE IS TO HATE IS TO LOVE IS TO HATE

The pantheist has said: Look at that tree; there you will find God. Look to the sky; in it is God. Look to the dust of the earth and the waters that fill the seas. These things also are God. God is me as he is also you. God is in all and is all. All is one, there is nothing else.

Pantheism is the philosophical position that asserts that God and the universe are essentially identical and that God is no more and no less than the collective stuff of the universe. While pantheistic views deny the existence of God in the traditional sense, they do offer a sort of divine presence in the universe: a god of which the universe is composed. God is not a separate being. He is not a living thing that can be differentiated from other things. Rather, God is ultimate reality. Since we, too, are ultimate reality, then we, too, are God. And so the pantheist would hold that the "universe as a whole is divine."[1]

Having declared the universe divine, the pantheist must then define what is meant by the term *universe*. After all, is divinity engrained within the physical matter of which the universe is composed? Or, could it be that matter is only illusion and that it is the spirit of the universe that is it fact divine? How can we differentiate between the two?

In his defense of pantheism John Hunt has answered that "since we neither know what matter is, nor what spirit is, it being impossible to demonstrate the existence of one apart from the other, the indefinite meaning of pantheism necessarily remains."[2] With this said, the terms

1. Harrison, *Elements of Pantheism*, 1.
2. Hunt, *Pantheism and Christianity*, 1.

universe and *God* may be used interchangeably. The universe, whether it is called matter or spirit, is one metaphysical divine unit.

For the pantheist, the fissiparous whole of humanity is nothing more than a single divine mass. This pantheistic divinity is represented within numerous religious traditions, ideologies, and philosophical outlooks. One thing that many pantheistic worldviews share in common is their commitment to the belief that each living thing is of the same spiritual substance as the universe as a whole. Such thinking is particularly evident in the non-dualistic religions of the East.[3] Pantheism is woven throughout such religions as Hinduism and Buddhism. This, of course, creates difficulty in presenting an accurate treatment of pantheism in its broad sense. James Sire has correctly noted that Eastern thought is extremely diverse and very difficult to "label and categorize."[4] I certainly do not wish to unfairly lump all Eastern religions and philosophies together under one common system, and so for the sake of finding an explanation for love I will search primarily those pantheistic systems whose traditions and beliefs are most widely and carefully developed.

A vast number of those who advocate Eastern pantheistic non-dualistic thought have placed their faith, their thought, their hope, and their eternities in these philosophies that assign divinity to the cosmos and transcendence to man.[5] On this metaphysical foundation are built the ethical principles relating to morals, to virtues, and ultimately to love. When questions of love arise, many pantheists will claim that love is possible. They will claim that love is a reality that must be lived out and enjoyed. Yet, can Eastern pantheistic non-dualism properly support and defend the rightness and goodness of love? To answer this question one need look no further than the most significant and oldest religious tradition in south Asia: Hinduism.

Hinduism is a "vast and diverse collection of related deities, practices, and philosophies."[6] It should be noted that within Hinduism there

---

3. *Non-Dualism* by definition may be equated with the term *Monism*. These terms refer to the oneness, and hence non-duality of the universe. All is one. Atman is Brahman. I am God, and God is I. There is essentially only one essence in the universe.

4. Sire, *Universe*, 147.

5. When I say "a vast number," I am referring to those who belong to the Advaita Vedanta system of Hinduism, as well as the followers of Theravada and Mahayana Buddhism, including Zen.

6. Harrison, *Elements of Pantheism*, 13.

are "almost no restrictions on personal beliefs."[7] All that is required for one to be counted among those within the Hindu tradition is acceptance of the Vedas, acceptance of the caste system, and the veneration of the deities and spirits.[8] This is why Hindus who are introduced to Islam or Christianity will often accept Allah, or Jesus as simply one more god among many.

In Advaita Vedanta Hinduism God is defined in pantheistic terms. There is no distinction between God and the individual. In other words the individual soul is the same as the universal soul. This idea is expressed in the Upanishads. Written around 600 B.C., these writings first introduced the proposition that Brahman is the unity of all things. Brahman, however, must not be confused with Brahma, the creator god. Rather, Brahman should be understood as an impersonal pantheistic form of God.[9] *Brahman*, the universal soul, is by nature of his essence, identical to *Atman*, the individual or world soul. Since each individual is ultimately equated with God, and God is the universe or cosmos, then this eliminates any distinction between God, the universe, and the individual. It is thought by many Hindus that "nothing whatsoever exists but the divine."[10] If there is anything that is not God, and yet, appears to exist, then it is only *maya*, or illusion.[11]

The significance of all this is that when one realizes his unity or oneness with Brahman, then that individual has passed beyond personality, beyond knowledge, beyond thought, beyond time, and beyond good and evil. Like a million colored pigments all mixed into the same glass of water, so stands the individual human in light of the universe. He is as much the universe as the universe is he.

To understand love in such a context one must first understand *karma*. In fact, love and hatred, and good and evil cannot be separated from karma in a pantheistic worldview. The idea of karma is quite simple; every past action has a future consequence. Harm done against

7. Corduan, *Neighboring Faiths*, 189.

8. The Vedas are the early sacred writings of the Aryan culture. These sacred writings include the Rig-Veda, the Yajur Veda, the Sama Veda, and the Atharva Veda. At times the commentaries known as the Upanishads have been included as part of the Vedas.

9. Corduan, *Neighboring Faiths*, 193.

10. Schiffman, *Sri Ramakrishna*, 153.

11. Sire, *Universe*, 146.

another can only bring future harm to the harmer. Sin is not canceled by forgiveness, nor by reparation. Rather, it is worked out in the next life. If I were to commit a vile and atrocious act toward another living thing, I may come back as a human in a lesser position, or as a beast, or as an insect. Actions committed in this life determine one's status in the next life. Like a mindless law of nature, so karma casts itself into the workings of the natural world. Like an ever watchful eye it sees the actions of the actor upon the stage. It is his audience. But unlike a play, the curtain stays open for life-time after life-time. The act is not finished easily.

All moral thought and action must be seen in context to this brutal critic. Love itself is subject to its laws, and these laws have ultimately eliminated the value of love. Remember that love is *a gift of genuine benevolence and of merciful goodwill, passionately displayed, and emanating from an altruistic concern.* Realize also that to love is to intervene morally in the life of another person. Such intervention may rather be interference. After all, to act kindly or benevolently toward anyone is to interfere with that person's karma. To act lovingly is to interfere with the other's suffering. For the Hindu, each of us suffers for a reason. We suffer because the deeds of a past life demand our suffering. With this in mind, one must realize that karma does not allow for any fundamental obligation or benefit to love.

If someone were suffering, it would be better not to interfere with this suffering. The injured party is injured as a result of his karma. To involve one's self with the karma of another, whether good or bad is to bring only more bad karma on both.

Furthermore, Brahman, the ultimate reality, is beyond good and evil. If I love, then I have no more loved than hated. If I do good, then I have done evil. Everything is good as everything is evil. To love is to hate, is to love, is to hate, *ad infinitum.* Selfishness, hatred, and murder are no more immoral than is love. Where then is love? Has its sweetness been dissolved as a lump of sugar in an ocean? Is it like a barren tree under the greyness of autumn where there were once green leaves and warm sun?

In pantheism the divinity of the universe will remain. If I kill something divine, and yet I remain, then divinity also remains. If I cease to exist, the cosmos will still remain, and thus, divinity will still remain. Good and evil can have no effect upon my ontological state. Likewise, love can have no affect upon it. Love cannot and must not exist; love cannot interfere with the divine cosmos.

Like Hinduism, certain forms of Buddhism share a belief in a pan-theistic universe and the governing ever watchful eye of karma, and like Hinduism, the Buddhist tradition does not see God and the universe in a traditional theistic sense. There is no creator. Everything that is has always been. Alan Watts has noted that, "Hindus and Buddhists pre-fer to speak of reality as 'non-dual' rather than 'one,' since the concept of one must always be in relation to that of many."[12] It must be noted that as there are many ways of practicing Hinduism, so also are there many different Buddhist traditions, such as Theravada (the small raft), and Mahayana (the large raft). While Theravada Buddhism emphasizes and elevates the position of the monks, allowing only the few devout to stand upon the raft, the Mahayana tradition has a broader acceptance of the masses, allowing all to climb aboard. Within the Mahayana tradi-tion one will find various divisions of Buddhist thought, including Pure Land, Tibetan, and Zen.

Since there is neither adequate room here, nor adequate need to ex-amine each of these schools of thought in detail, I will henceforth reserve my treatise on Buddhism to that of the widely held Zen tradition. It must be noted that Zen Buddhism is not identical to Hindu non-dualism. One major difference between these two is that followers of Zen do not devote themselves to veneration of a universal soul. For the Buddhist, ultimate reality is a non-sentient vacuousness whose essence cannot be abased by description. Yet, even if it is a "nothing" it is still a reality of sorts, and is, in its glorious void, a divine nothing. For this reason, even though advocates of Buddhism are often said to be atheistic, they still fall within the monism of pantheistic thought. Zen's attempt to distance itself from pantheism is not convincing.

Indeed, in spite of Zen master, D.T. Suzuki's, claims to the contrary, Zen fits the criteria of a pantheistic worldview. Suzuki claims that Zen does not deal with concepts. Rather, he says that it is nonsensical and un-intelligible.[13] Yet, Suzuki speaks of the *Self* in pantheistic terms saying:

> As this ultimate Self is above all forms of dichotomy, it is neither inner nor outer, neither metaphysical nor psychological, neither objective nor subjective. If the term "self" is misleading, we may

12. Watts, *Way of Zen*, 50.
13. Suzuki, *What is Zen*, 3–4.

designate it as "God" or "Being," "Man" or "the Soul," "Nothing" or anything.[14]

The "Self" of which Suzuki speaks is in fact, ultimate reality. This Self is masked behind antithetical language in order to render it unintelligible, yet, in spite of this, it is still an ultimate reality in which all things partake. There is no distinction between anything. Suzuki stated:

> The Ultimate Reality, whatever name we may give to it—the Self, the Mind, the Absolute, or God—is really a something or a nothing which is altogether beyond the grasp of a thinkable thinking agency. And at the same time it is graspable as such, as beyond our grasp, for to state something positive or negative about it makes it to that extent fall beyond human intelligibility.[15]

In Zen Buddhism a human being does not exist as a "separate individual."[16] The human being or self is unattainable. The mind is no-mind. There is no "substance or existence or being or subjectness…that can be definitively brought down to the intellectually analyzable level."[17] Suzuki explains that the "most important thing in the study of Zen is not to keep on riding on the donkey but to realize that you are the donkey itself, and in fact, the whole universe is the donkey."[18] The unintelligibility of this statement makes it clear that to hold such a position one must truly become the ass. But more seriously, I think what Suzuki is trying to say is that there is no beginning or end to the Self. The Self is all things and is only a moment in the greater scheme of things. The Self is the no-self, and yet the self must be done away with so that the no-self can be attained.

For the Buddhist, individual life in all its reincarnated states is like a small drop of water separating from a waterfall as it cascades down to the pool below. This drop of water is an individual separated from the larger body of water to which it belongs. It falls slowly changing physical form and shape as if undergoing many thousands of lifetimes, but eventually splashes into the pool, mixing with and being absorbed back into the whole. The individual drop will never be detected, it is now

14. Ibid., 10–11.
15. Ibid., 10–11.
16. Vroom, *No Other*, 16.
17. Suzuki, *What is Zen*, 22.
18. Ibid., 29.

one with the pool. In this way each human individual is like the drop of water undergoing a multitude of reincarnations in order to find his way back to the whole, and back to the ultimate reality from where he came. The no-self becomes the self, and must again become the no-self. The Self—the thinking, non-thinking, non-existent, exister, God, who is not God, who is there and not there to live and die and live and die and live—is the no-self.

This is certainly difficult for Western minds to understand. It appears as gibberish, without any meaning. Yet, for the Zen Buddhist, this is entirely the point.

The difficulty with the Buddhist understanding of the Self is that even if this Self must be done away with in order to attain to the no-self, it must be acknowledged that this Self does in some way exist. Even if it must be negated, there is still a Self, or Ego, or Someone who at some level exists in "relationship to others and thus has a separate individuality."[19] Even the enlightened person is still a being who acts, thinks, responds, and has responsibility within a community.[20] Though human beings exist together and in relationship to one another there is distinct individuality that cannot be philosophically denied. Surely I am not the same substance and being as everyone else. Can anyone read my thoughts or ideas as if reading a book? Can anyone comprehend my fears, my affections, and my love? Is love even possible within this Buddhist framework? Is love possible even for the great and enlightened one?

In defense of pantheistic philosophy, Alan Watts has claimed that there is no good or evil, they are both one.[21] Zen master, Masao Abe, reflects on good and evil saying, "my moral life resulted in the realization of the radical evil at the bottom of the fight between good and evil and my fundamental ignorance of the ultimate truth."[22] Humans are bound to radical evil if they cannot move beyond the difference between good and evil. And if there is no difference between good and evil then in fact there is no good or evil at all. Good and evil are illusory.

This would seem to make love illusory as well since love may be categorized under the banner of goodness. Yet, there is a notion of love

19. Vroom, *No Other*, 17.

20. Ibid., 18.

21. Watts, *Way of Zen*, 118.

22. Abe, *Zen*, 191.

within the Mahayana tradition of Buddhism. The word is *maitri* and translates as loving-kindness. There have been numerous stories involving the Buddha sacrificing himself in various ways for the love of others. In one of his pre-enlightenment lives it is said that after healing his wicked cousin, the Buddha was attacked by his cousin and fatally wounded. Since the Buddha did not harbor feelings of hatred against his cousin his fatal wound was closed up and he lived.[23] Many other legends involving the self-sacrificial love of the Buddha have circulated for centuries. Some of these acts of love are attributed to the Buddha "either during his final existence on earth, or, more particularly, during his earlier lives both human and animal."[24]

Henri du Lubac relates several legends surrounding the Buddha Sakyamuni. It is said that during his time upon the wheel of *samsara* the future Buddha had been reincarnated as a stag.[25] One tragic day his forest home became engulfed in flame. As the fire quickly spread, the animals were filled with great distress and fled as the fire encroached upon them. But soon they were halted by a great river with rushing torrents. Rather than face the heat of the raging fire, the animals began to throw themselves to the mercy of the river. Moved with pity the stag proceeded into the torrent and delivered the other animals from death. The water tore at him and crushed his bones, and yet he continued to save each animal until his strength failed, and he died.[26]

After a series of further reincarnations the future Sakyamuni Buddha was incarnated as the king of the Sibis. One day the god Indra decided to test the goodness of the king. He took the form of a hawk and pursued another god who was disguised as a dove. As the dove fled the hawk he took refuge in the king's bosom. Yet, the hawk, asserting his right to the dove, demanded that the king furnish either the dove or an equal portion of his own flesh. The king, moved with pity and selflessness, cut the flesh from his own body. Yet, the scale in which the dove had been placed continued to grow heavier, always outweighing the flesh

---

23. This story was related by Henri de Lubac in *Aspects*, 18.

24. Ibid., 20.

25. Samsara refers to the process by which each living thing must return after death until enlightenment has occurred. While various Eastern traditions view Samsara differently, the underlying principle is the same. In Hinduism this process is seen as reincarnation, while in Buddhism the term rebirth is preferred.

26. De Lubac, *Aspects*, 21.

that was meant to procure the dove's ransom. Finally, the king threw his entire body upon the scale to save the bird. The king had passed the test and Indra then granted him an even greater reincarnation.[27]

Such stories have moved many Buddhists to emulate these deeds of self-sacrifice and loving-kindness. Inspired by the Buddhas of old, some Buddhist monks have made a great effort to organize charitable social work. Yet, is the Buddhist who engages in such love truly living consistently with the teachings of Buddhism? Can the Buddhist religion support a desire to behave in self-sacrificial love?

Like Hinduism before it, Buddhism fails at love. The Buddhist has made it clear that the ego or individual person is illusory. To act self-sacrificially toward another, is to act self-sacrificially toward something that is not really there. This would be counterproductive since the ego exists only to later be destroyed.[28] And if this ego is mere illusion, then how can it be loved for itself? There is nothing there to love. The only benefit to love in such a situation is selfish gain.

Furthermore, consider the four noble truths of Buddhism and the emphasis they put on the elimination of desire:

1. To live is to suffer.

2. Suffering is caused by desire.

3. If desire is eliminated then so also will suffering be eliminated.

4. In order to accomplish this, one must follow the eightfold path.

The eightfold path consists of a series of requirements that involve behavior, thought, meditation and action. The significance of the four noble truths is found in the third truth. This is the elimination of desire.

Consider again the nature of love as *a gift of genuine benevolence and of merciful goodwill, passionately displayed, and emanating from an altruistic concern.* Love must involve not only a conscious act of concern for another human being but it must also involve a desire to act. The giving of benevolence and goodwill demands desire as a prerequisite. To love, one must necessarily desire to concern oneself with another. Love may be seen by the Buddhist as good, yet desire is seen as evil, or at least as unwanted. Both love and the need to eliminate desire are in

27. Ibid,. 21–22.

28. Ibid., 37.

constant contention with one another. To love is to desire, and to desire is to suffer. To suffer is to remain on the wheel of samsara, or rebirth. To love is counterproductive. If the Buddhist is to follow his own teaching consistently, then he is to be rid of desire and love along with it.

I once asked a Buddhist friend what love meant within the Buddhist tradition. He explained to me that it was not his place to interfere with morality. He looked at me and with all honesty in his voice said, "if I were to see an accident on the road in which a victim was in serious need of assistance, I could drive by in good conscience allowing that person to suffer and thus maintain what is duly allotted to him and to me. Or, I could stop and help which would spiritually benefit neither me nor the victim in any way."

Just as in Hinduism, karma has allotted to each the suffering he deserves. To help those who suffer is to bring further suffering. To love those who suffer is to irritate a wound, or to beat those who have fallen. To love is to hate is to love is to hate. Eastern pantheistic non-dualism offers us no explanation for love.

POLYTHEISM: THE MANY FACES OF LOVE

It is clear from examining pantheism that metaphysical systems will necessarily reflect upon ethical systems. The two cannot be divorced, either one from the other. In whatever way the universe is said to exist, morality will be a necessary part of that existing universe. As in atheism, pantheism offers no benevolent, merciful, or altruistic source, and therefore is unable to offer benevolence, mercy, or altruism. In pantheism, there is no duality and therefore love cannot be moved beyond hatred.

Since it is necessary to subject every philosophical outlook to questions of truth and livability, then I must not stop at pantheism. Polytheism, too, must be subjected to these same criteria if it is to be understood as a viable option. After all, polytheism makes metaphysical judgments about reality, and therefore, makes ethical judgments about reality. It is now polytheism's turn to dispense its sapience upon us as we continue to search for the explanation for love.

I remember as a child reading the ancient Greek myths of Hercules, Zeus, Athena and the many other gods, goddesses, and demigods who interacted in love and hatred, in peace and war, and in joy and sadness. These gods would carry on much like humans as they went about their jealous ways, whimsically living their lives, eating and drinking and partaking in every sort of merrymaking. It is true that most people have long forgotten these fatuous and infantile deifications and have dismissed these gods as myths. Yet, polytheism in its more developed forms remains a position that is accepted by many today as a valid and reasonable explanation of reality. The two most widely practiced forms of polytheism include Bhakti Hinduism and Mormon monarchotheism. The Mormon position will be defined and critiqued later but let us first examine Hindu polytheism.

Within the Hindu tradition, polytheism still prospers as worshippers devote themselves to the gods. Even within the New Polytheistic movement, there are those who have accepted plurality of both truth and gods over any one absolute system. Within this polytheistic society, even though one god may be worshiped at a time, the fact remains that many gods are worshiped.[29] According to many polytheists, monotheistic thinking has proved to be inadequate for dealing with the plurality of our world with its diversity of thoughts, and requirements, and its need for many gods.[30]

Hinduism remains the most significant source of polytheistic thought in the modern world. As I have stated earlier, there are many ways of practicing Hinduism. The Hindu practice most concerned with a polytheistic metaphysic is the "way of devotion." This form of Hinduism is largely interested in attachment to a god or many gods and goddesses. This school of thought has become known as Bhakti Hinduism, and is perhaps the most widely practiced within the Hindu world. Realize however, that even within the Bhakti tradition Hindus regard the world in a non-dualistic manner. They view Brahman as ultimate reality, and realize the Brahman Atman unity. However, such beliefs remain inconsequential to many Hindus who desire a relationship with a real living god.

For the Hindu polytheist, the concept of ultimate reality in the Advaita Vedanta tradition is far too transcendent and impersonal. Instead of trying to grasp the abstractness and intangibility of the Brahman Atman unity, Bhakti Hinduism clings to the service and veneration of gods. For this reason many Hindus view Brahman as manifesting itself in three gods: "Brahma, the creator; Vishnu, the preserver; and Shiva, the destroyer."[31] Though these are the three primary gods of Hinduism,

29. Miller, *New Polytheism*, 6, 58.

30. Ibid., 7.

31. Corduan, *Neighboring*, 200.

there are a great multitude of others as well. Among these are Ganesha, Krishna, Skandar, Lakshmi, and Kali. It is exaggerated that there are as many as 330 million gods and goddesses. Perhaps this is true, but if nothing else this number emphasizes the girth of the plurality of divinity in the universe.

Within Hindu polytheistic culture, ritual devotion is shown toward the deities. Such devotion was likewise present in ancient Egyptian, Greek, and Roman culture, and is clearly present in Indian culture today. Depictions of the gods are crafted, in which the gods themselves are thought to reside. These statues are bathed, fed, and clothed with great care and diligence as a parent cares for a child or as a son or daughter tends to a aging parent. Even the goddess Kali, whose appetite is for blood, must be satisfied by those thugs who would do her work upon the innocent.[32] That which each god demands must be given, for in each god lies the key to eternity. But, where does love enter the picture?

The Bhakti tradition emphasizes devotion to a god, and with this devotion, love. The god is worshiped and becomes the devotee's true and personal God. Within the Bhakti tradition there are eleven degrees of love for God that culminate ultimately in "perpetual self-effacement before God."[33] This self-effacement is a symbol that the devotee has "loved himself away in God."[34]

But how does this devotion manifest itself in Hindu thought? The story begins centuries ago when the *Samkhya* philosophy of dualism was widely practiced in India. The Samkhya tradition began by recognizing two dual realities in the universe which over the centuries have melded

---

32. Worshipers of the goddess Kali have traditionally worshiped her by offering human sacrifice. Those involved in the procurement of a suitable human sacrifice have been known as "thugs." Human sacrifices to Kali are still made occasionally in parts of India.

33. Dhavamony, 88. There are eleven degrees of love as mentioned by Dhavamony—1. Gunamahatma-asakti is attachment to God based upon his greatness. 2. Rupa-asakti is attachment to God's beauty. 3. Pujasakti is attachment to the worship of God. 4. Smaranasakti is the attachment to the memory of God. 5. Dasyasakti involves lifelong servanthood to God. 6. Sakhyasakti involves loving God as a friend. 7. Vatsalyasakti involves submissiveness to God. God is no longer simply a friend, but is loved on a much deeper level. 8. Kantasakti involves growth of familiarity with God. 9. Atmanivedana-asakti is the highest self-offering to God. God becomes the other self. 10. Tanmayasakti involves union with God. 11. Parama-viraha-asakti is the final stage of devotion to God. God and God alone is the only thing loved at this point. There is nothing beyond love of God. Even self-love is manifested in love for God.

34. Ibid,. 89.

into one monistic reality. Among these two interconnected realities is *parushas*, which is defined by all "individual, immaterial, eternal, and indestructible souls," and *prakriti*, which constitutes the corporeal material world with its three elements, or *gunas*.[35] Now, among the gunas of prakriti are *Sattva*, which is goodness and truth, *Raja*, which is passion and activity, and *Tamas*, which is darkness and inertia.[36] The physical world exists because these three elements of prakriti have fallen out of equilibrium.

As parushas interplay and mingle with prakriti the world will remain out of equilibrium, moving tumultuously from age to age until at last the gunas reach symmetry and balance and the world as we understand it vanishes once again. This infinite cycle will play itself out over and over again. Elliot Miller states that:

> The other important element in this drama is that the parushas become captive to prakriti. It is believed that out of a desire to understand the nature of prakriti they venture into it. As they come into contact with the material world, their pure consciousness generates mind and thought, which are believed to be part of prakriti and not proper attributes of parusha. The parushas' sensations and perceptions create false egos in which they believe they are part of the material world, and this belief entangles them in it. This bondage takes the form of transmission of individual souls from one body to another and ultimately reincarnation, once the parushas reach the human level.[37]

In other words, each human being is entangled in a false reality from which it must escape. This escape, or *moksha* from the world is accomplished through devotion to the gods, which plays out in the practice of yoga.

As in Buddhism, the meditational practices of Hindu yoga facilitate disengagement of all activities of the mind that are held captive by the physical world. Though Bhakti Hinduism is polytheistic, it is tied together by the belief in the ultimate oneness of Brahman. Thus, even with the recognition of a plurality of gods the duality of the parusha prakriti distinction melts away into the monistic realization that Atman is Brahman. Everything reduces to Brahman. The Bhakti tradition rec-

35. Miller, "Yoga Boom."
36. Ibid.
37. Ibid.

ognizes, therefore, this Ultimate Reality which springs from Brahman, yet meets the human need to worship a personal deity.

This personal element has attracted many to Bhakti Hinduism. The "cold, impersonal, and speculative" aspects of Brahmanism are done away with as the worshiper focuses his love and devotion on Shiva, Krishna, or others. Just as the devotee loves his god, so also, is the devotee loved by his god. There is a mutual and perpetual love that is engrained in and permeates the relationship. Where pure non-dualistic pantheism fails to provide a basis for love, "the way of devotion" delivers.

With this said, is it possible that I have found an explanation for love in polytheism? Is it possible that the impersonal Brahman has created personal love and devotion through the existence of gods and men? Bhakti Hinduism brings us nearer to love than before but still falls short of an adequate explanation.

When considering love within a polytheistic context several problems arise. First, Brahman cannot be a necessary cause. It cannot create out of nothing. It cannot be self existing. Consider an earthen pot. "Clay is its material cause, the wheel its instrumental cause, and the potter its efficient cause."[38] Yet, who caused the clay, and the wheel? Who created them? In essence, who is the necessary cause? The Hindu Rig-Vedas claim that in the beginning "there was neither nonexistence nor existence."[39] Brahman, the One, was there only by its impulse. The Rig-Vedas go on to say that "desire came upon that One."[40] From desire came mind. But where did this desire come from if mind was not there first? Creation is said to have come before the gods appeared. The following is said in Hindu Scripture: "Where this creation has arisen—perhaps it formed itself, or perhaps it did not—the One who looks down on it, in the highest heaven, only he knows—or perhaps he does not know."[41] Unlike theism, which asserts that there is a God who is eternal, who exists outside of time and space, and who operates as a first and necessary cause, polytheism creates an infinite regress. If not from Brahman, then from where did things come? If not from Brahman, then from where did personality, desire, and mind arise? Everything is Brahman. Does everything self-

38. Ibid., 225.

39. *Rig-Veda* 10.129; *Brihad-Aranyaka Upanishad* 1.4.1–7. Taken from Van Voorst, *Anthology*, 32.

40. Ibid., 33.

41. Ibid., 33.

exist? If Brahman is a non-personal and non-thinking reality then from where do personality and thought and creativity come? Such questions will be asked *ad infinitum*. There is no answer. If God is bound in such an infinite regress, then love and morality are bound as well.

Likewise, Hindu polytheism reverts to pantheism. In the Hindu tradition there is a place from where all gods and goddesses come. They come ultimately from Brahman, for Brahman is everything. Yet, if all things issue from Brahman, or are equated with Brahman, then love or devotion to God means nothing, because the devotee ends up again with pantheism. If a god is Brahman, and Brahman is everything, and I belong to that which is everything, then there is no distinction between me or Brahman or a god. Where pantheism fails at love, so also does polytheism.

Furthermore, Hindu polytheism is forced to define love in a very weak sense. There can be no definitive meaning to love. Love must mold and conform itself capriciously since its definition depends upon both the god and the devotee. If I have devoted my love to the goddess Kali then my actions will demonstrate my love for her. Perhaps I will offer a human sacrifice as a means of showing her my love and devotion. Yet, if I am devoted to Vishnu, my love will be demonstrated in a very different way. In a broader sense, one may devote himself to Baal, or Zeus, or Satan. In the worship of Satan love would be defined as pure hedonism, and self-gratification. This relativistic and pluralistic inability to define love has already been shown to fail, leaving polytheism defunct and vacuous.

These many faces of love fall short. Hindu polytheism offers no legitimate source of love, and fails to give any explanation for why self-sacrificial altruistic goodwill directed toward others ought to exist. Yet, Hindu polytheism is not the only multi-deity religion that offers a solution. We now turn to Mormon monarchotheism.

MONARCHOTHEISM: GOD, GODS, AND THE PLIGHT OF LOVE

The concept of God or gods in the Mormon worldview is not only very different from that of Hindu polytheism but in many ways difficult to clearly define. Mormon theogony, or study of God's origin in the universe, remains in a certain state of unrest as new revelations by Mormon leadership are adding to what is already stated about God in the large body of Mormon writings. Yet, to simply lump the Mormon view of God together with Hindu polytheism would do great injustice to a highly developed Mormon theological system. It is worth, therefore, our efforts to distill away any obfuscation concerning the Mormon worldview so that it may be more easily examined as a tenable explanation for the existence of love in the universe. Perhaps then, Mormon monarchotheism will move me closer to the answers I seek.

The term *monarchotheism* has been used by philosophers to describe "the theory that there is more than one God, but one God is clearly preeminent among the gods; in effect, he is the monarch or ruler of all the gods.[42] Contemporary Mormon theology, therefore, tends to view God not merely as the God of this world, but as the God who is not subordinate to any other God in the universe.[43] Having derived certain aspects of its theology from Christian scriptures, Mormonism shares some similarities with traditional Christian interpretations of God's character and morality. However, when asking specifically about the ontology of God, the Mormon position strays immensely from the orthodox Christian position.

For example, though Christians and Mormons can agree that God is personal, Mormons add that he is also embodied. Joseph Smith, the founder of Mormonism, asserts, "there is no other God in heaven but that God who has flesh and bones."[44] This embodied deity, who is essentially an exalted man, is not the creator of the world but rather the organizer of preexisting material.[45] The universe exists in spite of God, but without him would be subject to chaos. The God of Mormonism is therefore contingent upon the universe. This is to mean that God is not necessary. He might very well not exist at all. Such a God does not need to exist as God but might exist as some other being: a man, an angel, or a unicorn.

As little more than an exalted man, God is limited in his knowledge of future events and is limited in his ability to express any power outside of the dimensions of space and time.[46] God is therefore finite

---

42. Parrish, "Tale of Two," 195. It should also be noted that Kretzmann is credited with first using the term "monarchotheism" in his book *God of the Bible*.

43. Ibid., 200.

44. Smith, *Teachings*, 181.

45. *Book of Mormon*, Abraham 3:24; 4:1–3.

46. Smith, *Teachings*, 385. Smith is reported to have said that "God himself was once as we are now, and is an exalted man . . ."

in a physical sense, yet at the same time infinite as one who in spirit form has always existed. Though Mormons believe that God is infinite in his existence, they do not believe that he is the basis for ethical value. Many Mormon scholars hold that God's ethical standard is subject to something outside of himself.[47]

Imagine if you will, a very wise and very moral man who is given the opportunity to reside over the affairs of the entire world. He is given superhuman powers and knowledge, and is able to live for an infinite amount of time as he governs the earth. He is superior to any other living thing in the universe, and is able to do almost anything he pleases. He can fly, he can lift astronomically large rocks over his head and throw them through the air, and he can know what everyone is thinking at this precise moment. In many ways this caricature resembles the God of Mormonism.

This stands in sharp contrast to the classical Christian view of God which emphasizes one who is immaterial, sovereign, self-existing, and unique as the only such being in existence. Classical Christian theism also affirms God's omniscience, omnipotence, omnipresence, and transcendence as one who is external to the universe of space and time. God, in this view, is also immutable, eternal, and immanent. In contrast to Mormon theism, classical Christian theism also holds that God is the source of goodness.

Mormon theology diverges greatly from both Islamic and Judeo-Christian monotheism by holding to a plurality of gods. While Christian monotheism defends the existence of one triune God whose essence exists in three individual persons, Mormon monarchotheism defends a form of tritheism, asserting that the Godhead is made up of three separate personages. These three gods, the Father, the Son and the Spirit, share their purpose and power, but are three separate entities.[48]

However, Mormon theism does not stop with three gods. Smith believed that all human beings have existed infinitely in the same way that God has existed infinitely. We are thus co-eternal and co-existent with the Father himself. The spirit or intelligence of man has no beginning.[49] In addition to this, Smith earlier proclaimed with even greater audacity,

---

47. See Parrish, *New Mormon*, 200–203.

48. Ibid., 203.

49. Smith, *Teachings*, 352–54.

that God was once as humans are now.[50] God is therefore, little more than a man, and men are little less than unactualized gods. The God of Mormonism is not even thought to be the original God. He had a father before him, and his father was the offspring of yet another. If Hinduism purports the existence of 330 million gods, then Mormonism has far outdone even it. In fact, one may be inclined to suppose that there are indeed an infinite number of gods who through celestial procreation bequeathed godhood to the subsequent generation through eternity past.[51] The number of gods in the Mormon pantheon would therefore make Hindu polytheism look meager in comparison.

There are a number of problems with Mormon theogony, Mormon cosmology, and Mormon metaphysics in general, but my main concern here is with Mormon ethics and the Mormon explanation of the existence of love in the universe. One test of the validity of the Mormon worldview will be its ability to adequately defend its ethical position as relating most specifically to love.

As mentioned before, Mormon ethics does not derive universal value from God. The Mormon God is bound to an overarching moral law that is over and above him. As a contingent being, he is subject, rather than foundational, to any kind of absolute moral law. God was once a man who grew in moral knowledge and who was nurtured in moral insight. Even if he was always good on some level, his goodness is now even better than before. He has gained greater goodness and has procured moral superiority in his abounding love. The God of Mormonism like his God before him learned love from a moral code that has always been.

Having severed God from the moral code, and having made him subject to it, Mormonism has inflicted irreparable damage on its explanation for love in the universe. Allow me to explain. The gods of Mormonism are subject to a morality that is beyond them. They are subject to rules that they are obligated to obey. But like any obligating statute to which one is bound, such a code must have an author. If not, how can there be any obligation to live under its governance?

50. Ibid., 345–46.

51. Since the universe never had a beginning, and each Father had a Father before him, it is reasonable to conclude that the number of Mormon gods constitutes an actual infinity. Though many Mormons deny the infinite regress of gods that necessarily follows from Smith's teaching, this would seem to be the best logical outcome of the Mormon belief in an infinite number of infinite spirit beings.

Mormons claim that God is sovereign over his people. This sovereign authority has power to instruct his citizens according to his ethical law. But as Francis J. Beckwith asks in his critic of Mormon moral law, what if someone were to object and ask the sovereign why his moral law must be obeyed?[52] According to Beckwith, the sovereign now has three possible responses. He can (a) look to his own authority as sovereign, (b) appeal to another sovereign above himself, or (c) point to the authority of a moral law book that has existed always and that has no author.

If (a) is selected, one might then demand to know why the sovereign possesses such authority. The sovereign can either respond by claiming that he has always had moral authority, or he can point to another who is sovereign over him. The first option will not do, because as we have seen, the Mormon sovereign was not always that way. He was a man who received the moral law from another. He is therefore forced to point to another sovereign above him for his authority which leads to option (b).

As the sovereign appeals to *his* superior sovereign as the basis for his moral authority, his sovereign must either appeal to another sovereign above him, or conclude with option (c). If he appeals to another sovereign, one is left to fathom the logical impossibility of an infinite regress because every sovereign was once a man and cannot be the source of the moral law. Yet, an infinite regress is not tenable and must be discarded. One must, therefore, conclude with the existence of a moral law book as stated in option (c).

The problem with option (c) is that it forces two major difficulties. First, why should anyone trust the moral law book that no one has ever seen, including the sovereign himself? In other words, how do we know that what he says about love is trustworthy and true? Could I truly be expected to believe in a book that no one has ever read, and that no one has ever seen? Could I bring myself to believe this book that has communicated nothing to no one? After all, it is a book with no author, and has never been printed, bound, or read aloud. It does not even exist as an idea in a mind.

Secondly, how can a moral law book exist if it has no author? It would seem that someone must be responsible for such a book? If the moral law is a "free-floating" platonic form, why should anyone feel moral obligation to it, or guilt in opposing it?[53] The moral law is dis-

---

52. Beckwith, "Moral Law," 229.
53. Ibid., 230.

connected from a moral mind. Yet, rules exist because they are written. Virtues are virtues because they are declared as such. Love is real because it is given and received. A moral law without an author is no more than a song without sound, without notes, without thematic development, without harmonization, phrasing, modulation, texture, form, or mellifluous beauty.

If the moral code is not the result of mind, then is it perhaps the result of unthinking nature? Mormons believe that nature has existed infinitely in time and in space. Though God ordered and arranged it, it is not his creation. In the same way, the moral law has also existed somehow infinitely in time and in space. God is subject to the moral law as an object on earth is subject to the laws of gravity. In the same way, the moral law is a part of infinite nature and is therefore subject to it. Existing independently of any mind, the moral law can be nothing more than something evolved; it can flow from nothing more than an unthinking, unfeeling, and non-active mother.

In this way, the Mormon ethical system reduces to that of naturalism. Before there was God there was man, and before there was man there was matter. From matter came life, from life came genetic dispositions, and from these came God and a man made morality. The mind boggling infinite regresses and unattainable moral law books leave the Mormon explanation of love infinitely removed from humanity. For the Mormon, there are only two possibilities: to abandon the unattainable law book in favor of naturalism and its truculent selfishness, or to seek a God whose very nature is love and goodness.

The God of love must be a God who is eternally and perfectly good.[54] Such a God must love not because he declares love to be good but because he *is love*.[55] Such a God must not be "subject to a moral order outside of himself," neither must his moral decrees be arbitrary or prone to chance.[56] The God of love must be one who is morally free to exercise his love in any number of loving ways, according to his will, and yet he must be necessarily loving. The source of love must be a perfect and eternal source. Since love exists and is evident within humanity, I must now look to monotheism as a possibility for a better explanation

---

54. Ibid,. 232.

55. Ibid,. 232. Adapted from Beckwith's argument for good.

56. Ibid., 232.

of love. My multitude of religious and philosophical options has faded away to nearly nothing but still I seek to find love's source.

Allow me, if you will, to take you back to the game of senses mentioned earlier. The player had used all available information to make a reasonable decision about which item was indeed the roast beef. Now clearly all the items shared some things in common with the roast beef. Each was made of physical material. Each had extension in time and space. Each could be digested with varying amounts of intestinal pain or pleasure. Yet, only one was the true roast beef dinner. In many ways naturalism is like the shoe that the player first encountered. It reeks of inability to explain love, or any other form of goodness. Its flavor is bitter, lacking the seasoning of truth. Its attempt to borrow love from other worldviews renders it a gastronomic calamity.

Likewise, pantheism is like the bowl of steam. But steam lacks any true substance. If love is in there somewhere, it will never be found. Pantheism's promise of love is vaporous and inedible. There is no nourishing or nutritive explanation of love therein. It is closer to food than atheism, but not close enough to satisfy.

Polytheism, in both Hindu and Mormon form, is the plaster imitation of the true roast beef dinner. It offers a glimpse of something more tangible, something more joyous, and something more real. It tries to promise a divine source for love but falls far short. Man cannot live on imitation food. It may look real but only whets the appetite for something more. Yet, what more could there be? Has theism anything to offer?

4

The Eternal Source

Love and the Monotheist

IMAGINE A YOUNG BOY, full of energy and life, playing with a ball in the street behind his home and throwing the ball again and again into the air to see how high it will go. He hopes it will reach the sky, and he entertains himself for some time with this activity until at once he throws it through a window, shattering the glass, startling the dog, and upsetting a potted plant in the parlor. Immediately his mother descends on him in stern rebuke for his carelessness and speaks the words that every child dreads: "just wait until your father gets home!" Of course she leaves the mess of broken glass and pottery, as well as the now catatonic plant, as evidence of the boy's mischief. Now, he can only wait. The clock ticks on slowly and the boy remains to face the impending doom of punishment. He dares not even touch the ball and wishes he could return to some earlier moment before this all happened. Then he hears it; the door opens as his father returns home. Still, he waits as he hears through the wall the muffled voices of his mother and father. He rehearses once more all of his excuses, and in walks his father. But his father says nothing. In his right hand he carries a small broom, in his left a dustpan. He kneels down and cleans up every shard of glass and bit of dirt from the floor. Finally, he turns to the boy, hands him his ball, and says, "I, too, was once a child."

This image is one of grace, of mercy, of compassion, and most importantly, of love. In fact, this is the picture that the three great monotheistic religions paint of God, the good and loving Supreme Being who extends his compassion to a weak and finite humanity. With this said, it is only reasonable to explore these monotheistic religions, one of which may offer greater coherence in explaining love's origin, its presence in the world, and its reason to be. Atheism has failed to explain love, as have the various forms of pantheism and polytheism. Yet, love exists, and so we turn to monotheism as the logical next step.

The three great monotheistic traditions are recognized as Judaism, Christianity, and Islam. Even though there exist great similarities between the three, there are also profound differences. The main body of difference lies between Islam and the Judeo-Christian position. In the following pages I shall reduce the three into two and combine the thoughts of Jewish and Christian tradition, given that Christianity also assumes and absorbs the Jewish Scriptures.

LOVE AND THE UNITY OF GOD

From the walls of the synagogue, the mosque, and the cathedral, echo one significant teaching that lies foundational to monotheism, and that is the unity of God. "Hear, O Israel: The Lord our God, the Lord is one."[1] "He is God alone, God the eternal, he does not beget and he is not begotten. There in none co-equal with him."[2] There is "one God and Father, who is over all . . ."[3]

These statements taken from the Torah, the Qur'an, and the New Testament all bear witness to the unity of God. Both Christians and Muslims affirm the existence of this one all powerful Creator-God. Yet, conceptually, there are vast differences between Christianity and Islam in the perception of the person and nature of God.

Linguistically, Christians refer to this Supreme Being as God, while Muslims refer to him as Allah. However, for these two religions to speak of God is to speak of the same subject in different predicates.[4] This verbal avouchment differs while the basic subject remains the same. After all, the term Allah is no more than a word in the Arabic language used to refer to that which in the English language is called God.

The word itself, therefore, is of little consequence. It is the deeper meaning behind the word that is our ultimate concern. Take the word water as an example. Such a word refers to many things. To one it brings

1. Deuteronomy 6:4.

2. Qur'an 112. All citations of the Qur'an are taken from Maulana Muhammad Ali's English translation and commentary.

3. Ephesians 4:6.

4. Cragg, *Call*, 36–37.

thoughts of a vast tumultuous brine-ridden mass of waves colliding upon the shore. Yet, to another it is a gentle trickle bringing refreshment from thirst. So it is with that ambiguous utterance of divine epithet. The word God will have a much different meaning for the Muslim than for the Christian. And when speaking of the unified God it is the concept of unity that reveals the greatest difference between the Christian and Muslim.

The Islamic tradition is founded upon the affirmation of God's unity. In fact, there is nothing more paramount within Islam than the expression of the unity of God. An individual need only confess this unity in order to become a Muslim by sincerely stating: "La Ilaha Illa Allah"—there is no god except God.[5] This statement is the confirmation of Allah's lordship and supremacy. By uttering this statement, one pronounces the annihilation of all other deities.

Though a degree of supremacy was acknowledged of Allah in pre-Islamic Arabia, it was Muhammad who finally deposed the lesser deities and proclaimed Allah as exalted. This may also explain why the *Shahada* or confession is stated in a negative form. There is no lesser god, only Allah. To contend against this principle and assert the existence of other gods or to elevate other gods to equal status with God is known to Muslims as the sin of *shirk*. This is the unpardonable sin. God has no associates, no equals, and no partners, and there is absolutely nothing that ranks near him in power, majesty, and knowledge.

If one were to ask a Muslim to explain the doctrine of God in one word, it may likely be this: *unity*. God and idolatry are completely incompatible. This is why Muhammad, upon his entrance into Mecca, had all idols destroyed and the city cleansed of idolatry. With the existence of only one God, there was no need for these useless obscenities crafted of clay, and silver, and gold. There is no equal to God and there is no duality. Even God's name, *Allah*, is a proper name, which is itself, "grammatically incapable of a plural."[6]

God's unity is not only defended theologically within Islam, it is also argued for through philosophical reasoning. Because of certain metaphysical presuppositions, Islamic philosophers have consistently viewed unity as superior to plurality. This elevation of unity over plural-

---

5. This confession is known as the *Shahada*, and is all that is required for one to be considered a Muslim.

6. Cragg, *Call*, 39.

ity was also evident in the thinking of the Greek philosopher Plotinus several centuries before Muhammad brought the teaching of God's unity to the people of Arabia. According to historian of philosophy F.E. Peters, it is almost certain that Arabia had been exposed to "two different strains of Platonism: the Neo-Platonic version of Plotinus and Proclus, and the older Platonism taught in the Roman schools during the second and third century."[7] Within two centuries of the introduction of Islam, Muslim theologians were propagating Platonic and Neo-Platonic views of God with qur'anic support.[8] Early medieval philosophy was often entrenched in Neo-Platonism, evident not only in the qur'anic view of God, but in Christian theological and philosophical views as well, including those of St. Augustine.

The significance of this is that Plotinus viewed all plurality to flow from unity. Given this stance, unity must naturally be considered superior to plurality. The perfect God must be unified, because as plurality is introduced so also is evil. This is why virtue and right moral conduct are a concern for the plurality of individual humans but unnecessary for God.[9] He is beyond such things. As the infinite expanses of the universe are beyond human reach so also is plurality beyond the Muslim God.

Though the idea of the unity of God is shared between Muslims and Neo-Platonists, Islam diverges from Neo-Platonism in many other areas within epistemology and ethics. On this point Islam also diverges from the Christian concept that God exists in a triune form. The strict monotheism of Islam contends that such a Trinity would compromise God's absolute oneness. It would dilute him as if mixing in some contaminating element. It would ruin him as if making a king into a commoner. It would be like polluting pure wine with water.

In strictly upholding the unity of God in a Neo-Platonic manner, Muslims may find it odd and ironic that Christians defend the Trinity as a single unified God. Yet, Christians boldly assert that there is only one God who is Lord, Creator, and Sustainer of all things. In studying the first four of the Ten Commandments it is clear that they affirm, four essential principles. They affirm, firstly, the oneness of God in that he alone is God; secondly, the absolute quality of God in that no other god

---

7. Peters, "Origins of Islamic Platonism," 36.

8. These theologians include Jahm ibn Safwan, and Zakariyya al-Razi as related in "Origins of Islamic Platonism."

9. Holmes, *Fact, Value, God*, 44.

can replace, abrogate, or equal him; thirdly, the holiness of God in that his name is set apart in its uniqueness and status above false gods; and fourthly, the respect and honor due this one true God. Jesus himself later confirmed this truth by declaring that the greatest commandment is to love the Lord with one's entire heart, soul, and mind.[10] This command requires there be no division of the affection. God alone is to be loved and honored. To love anything else to this extent is to replace God and demote him.

Though Christians acknowledge the oneness of God, they have come to understand God's existence by explaining him as a Trinity. Contrary to the Islamic view of the Trinity in Surah 4:171 that speaks of a Father, Mother, and Son, Christians affirm God as the Father, Son, and Holy Spirit.[11] Biblical witness affirms that there are three persons who exist as one God. Each of these persons carries on differing roles within the Godhead. The Father is God who creates, sustains, and sends the Son to redeem humanity, whereas the Son is God who saves and judges the souls of man. Philippians 2:6 states that Christ Jesus "did not consider equality with God something to be grasped." What this affirms is that Jesus is equal in essence with God the Father. John 1 also states that Jesus existed "in the beginning," just as God did. He was there *sans* creation, and was himself the creator. Finally, references to the Holy Spirit confirm his equality with God. Acts 5:3–4 speaks of God and the Holy Spirit interchangeably. When Ananias and Sapphira lied to the Holy Spirit, it was said also that they were lying to God. Similarly, 1 Corinthians 3:16–17 states that the human body is a temple of God indwelt by the Holy Spirit. Again, the Holy Spirit is equated with God. God is one and yet he is three.

Even Christian theologians will observe that "on the surface, these two lines of evidence—God's oneness and threeness—seem contradictory."[12] Muslims are quick to agree. Yet, the Christian will defend this concept as not only biblical but logically sound. Second Corinthians 13:1 affirms all three persons in a single verse, linking "the three names

10. See Matthew 22:34–40.

11. Qur'an 4:171. Muslims have often confused the Trinity as consisting of the Father, Son, and Mary. This false trinity resembles something similar to the gods of mythology but is ontologically very different to the Trinity proposed by Christianity. This mistaken trinity demonstrates that though Mohammad was aware of many Christian ideas, he lacked a true understanding of Christian doctrine.

12. Erickson, *Introducing Christian*, 99.

in unity."[13] This unity found in the Trinity is no more illogical than the unity found in Allah. Christians are not stating that one God is equal to three Gods. They are not stating that colorless green ideas sleep furiously.[14] They are not claiming to lack vocal chords while speaking. Instead, they are stating that one substance exists in three persons. Essentially, one substance is *equal* to three persons. Though Muslims will show that the Trinity involves a mathematical error as 1+1+1=1, Christians may respond by demonstrating that 1x1x1=1. Mathematical equations do little to clarify the issue. God is triune, not triplex.[15] Christian theologians Bruce Demarest and Gordon Lewis affirm the triune God by stating:

> God is one substantially (one spiritual being) and one essentially (one spiritual being with all the attributes belonging to him). (Essence = Substance + Attribute). The unity is not merely a genus, for there are not three gods of the same kind (genus). Only a substantial and essential oneness fits the scriptural data denying polytheism and affirming monotheism. The divine unity revealed in Scripture is not like a mystical Neo-Platonic "One" beyond all categories of human thought. The biblical oneness does not rule out distinguishable attributes and persons.[16]

In concurrence with Demarest and Lewis, it must be added that the Trinity does not violate the law of non-contradiction. Now, this law of logic affirms that a statement and its negation cannot both be true. For example, it cannot be true that the earth orbits the sun if it is true that the earth does not orbit the sun. This is an obvious contradiction. The Trinity is not a belief in three essences in one essence, or three natures in one nature.[17] This, too, is obviously a contradiction. Rather, the Trinity exists as three persons in one essence. Norm Geisler uses several diagrams to demonstrate the validity of the Christian Trinity.[18] In one diagram Geisler identifies the three persons of the Trinity as: Father (who-1), Son (who-2), and Spirit (who-3). There are three *whos*, and one *what* (God). Therefore, each who is what.

---

13. Ibid., 100.

14. This phrase was used by Noam Chomsky in his *Syntactic Structures* to demonstrate the absurdity of semantic nonsense.

15. Geisler and Saleeb, *Answering Islam*, 269.

16. Demarest and Lewis, *Integrative Theology*, 271.

17. Geisler and Saleeb, *Answering Islam*, 272.

18. See Geisler and Saleeb, *Answering Islam*, 271–76.

A second diagram may further clarify the concept of the Trinity. The Father is not the Son, is not the Spirit, but is God. The Son is not the Spirit, is not the Father, but is God. The Spirit is not the Father, is not the Son, but is God. Each person is not the other person, but is God.

Though difficult to grasp, this Christian concept of the Triune God affirms that God is one and only one. As in Islam, there is only one God and this one God is unified. He is the absolute. He is that to which all things owe their existence.

Yet, the question remains: is it the Islamic or Christian concept of God's unity that best explains love? If love is yet to be explained by either an atheistic, pantheistic, or polytheistic source, then what is left but a divine eternal source? Upon examining the two diverse concepts of God within the Islamic and Christian traditions, it is the second of these two that posits a clearer elucidation of the origin of love.

Recalling that the Islamic view of God is based upon a rigid Neo-Platonic unity, the Qur'an itself affirms the absolute oneness of God. In Neo-Platonism, the *One* did not even know itself because self-knowledge requires both a *knower* and a *known* which in turn requires division.[19] Plotinus' One could only know itself by its effects on those things around it. It had no essence. In the same way, the Qur'an teaches that the essence of God is unknowable, if not inexistent. After all, God is both merciful, compassionate, and good, as well as damaging, tyrannical, and arrogant.[20] These attributes of God's essence would only contradict each other if God did indeed have an essence. Yet, they do not contradict, because as far as Islam is concerned, God does not have an essence, but exists as pure will. For the Muslim, even essence detracts from God's unity. Therefore, it can only be concluded that within the Islamic worldview, God is not by his nature loving, since he has no nature. Furthermore, if God is absolute unity, then it only follows that his ability to love becomes dependent upon those whom he loves. He cannot love until he has created something to love.

On the contrary, the Christian position affirms love as part of God's essence. First John 4:16 establishes that "God is love." Because this is so, the Christian God can love as a triune God, while Allah of Islam needs his creation in order to communicate love. As Francis Schaeffer has acknowledged, "God does not need the universe as the universe needs

19. Ibid., 270.
20. Cragg, *Call*, 43.

him."[21] Christians recognize the existence of a unified yet triune God, and in doing so recognize that "the persons of the Trinity communicated with each other and loved each other before the creation of the world."[22] Because of this, love can freely flow both between the persons of the Trinity, and from these persons to human beings.

LOVE AND THE NATURE OF GOD

If a woman were to describe the man who meets her ideal criteria for a mate, she would likely be concerned with his intellect, his charm, his generosity, his integrity, and his esteem and respect for his beloved. One would hardly expect her to spend her days dreaming about the molecular structure of her future husband. One would hardly expect her to dream of falling in love with a corporeal substance, who exists in time and who extends in space. In fact, it is absurd to think that she dreams of falling in love with a thing that moves about from place to place, responds to verbal prompting, and exhibits resemblance to other human life forms. Ultimately, she would not be concerned with *what* he is but with *who* he is. The question of *what* refers only to the fact that he is a man. The question of *who* refers to the characteristics that set him apart from others and qualify him as worthy of the woman's affection.

The difference in the Muslim and Christian concept of the divine does not simply end at the problem of unity. This question of unity begins to explain what God is but it does not adequately explain who God is. This question of unity informs us of the substance of God, his personhood, and his existence, but if anyone wishes to deeply and truly know the Lord of the universe then it is necessary to ask one very important question: "who is this God?" By asking this question, many following questions arise and provide content with which to understand this divine being and the love he exhibits to humans. By asking who God is, we must also ask what is the nature of this God? What are his character traits? Can we trust him? How does he behave?

When considering such questions, we must turn again to the two monotheistic options with the hope that one of these will provide an answer. A proper answer is vital here because where there are two options in the realm of worldviews, there must also be a decision. This

21. Schaeffer, *He is There*, 14.
22. Ibid., 14.

must be made clear before we can go any further, because as we have already seen, Islam and Christianity do not reduce to the same basic belief system.

Robert Frost opens his famous and oft quoted poem "The Road Not Taken," with a very lucid consideration about the nature of decisions by speaking of the divergence of two roads in a yellow wood. He then offers his sentiments of sorrow knowing he cannot travel them both. Those who know this poem return to it again and again because of the psychological, sentimental, epistemic, and ethical challenges it offers on the nature of choice and volition. We like to think of ourselves as the one, who after careful reflection, steps out on the road less travelled. Yet here our concern is not with the amount of foot traffic that has been inflicted upon either road; our concern, rather, is with the truth of the two responses with which we are faced. The significance of any such divergence of paths is that there is now an immediate and crucial option. A decision must be made.

As we examine the Christian and Islamic views of God we have an option that requires a decision. We have here a "yellow wood" of sorts, in that the road of metaphysical consideration has diverged and leads toward two differing outcomes. One path will lead to an Islamic under-standing of God's attributes, and the other to a Christian explanation. The significance in the diverging paths is that a decision *must* be made. Both paths cannot be taken, and it is not reasonable to simply stop and go no further, without hope of satisfying our need to know. When Frost faced a diverging path he could not simply stop and linger eternally at the junction. Nor could he return home. He made a decision and fin-ished his poem by reminiscing on his verdict and acknowledging that the one made was right. Yet, he could only guess. He had to go on his instinct. He did not necessarily choose wisely, but he did guess well. As man embarks on this path to discover the truth of God's nature he, too, must not guess but, rather, examine evidence and choose accordingly. There is far too much at stake for human beings to simply guess, and there is too much knowledge available to them to simply treat the matter as a triviality. Therefore, let us pursue insight into who God is, and let us determine if love is something that truly and freely flows from God.

Love exists. If monotheism is able to adequately explain love's ex-istence then it must provide an answer to the question of love's origin; it must explain how love translates from God to human beings; it must describe a God who is not only capable of love, but who freely demonstrates love. Since both Islam and Christianity offer differing views of God and his love, then, once more, it is necessary to seek an understanding of the nature of God as portrayed in each of these worldviews.

As Islam affirms God's unity, it also affirms his many marvelous actions and abilities. Among these capacities rests God's divine love demonstrated in mercy and compassion. All but one of the surah's of the Qur'an begin with the statement *Bismillah al-Rahmān, al-Rahīm*. This statement is one of the most vivid and essential statements in the Muslim faith, as it describes the way in which God relates to those who love him. This epitome of Muslim worship commonly translates: In the name of God, the Compassionate, the Merciful. Yet, as Kenneth Cragg has noted, the terms *Rahmān* and *Rahīm* derive from the same verbal root.[23] This means that one of the two adjectives ought to be understood as a noun. One term names God and the other describes the action appropriate to the name. Thus, God is not simply merciful, he is "the Merciful Mercier."[24] He is not simply compassionate, he is "the Compassionate Compassionator."[25] These statements would seem then to present God as one who has a nature of compassion and mercy.

If this is so, then so God also would possess other characteristics that describe his nature. When he is described in Surah 11:90 and 92 as *al-Wadud*, the loving, this would not only be a descriptor of God's divine prerogative to love, it would seem to speak more greatly to his nature as a loving God. Surah 85: 14–16 speaks also of God's love but adds a condition that must not be ignored. That vital condition is this: God is the "Doer of what he intends."[26] The emphasis here is on God's will, and not on his nature. In fact, many Muslim theologians will agree that the Qur'an is not a discourse on God's essence or nature but a treatise on God's function or actions in the universe.[27] Love may be considered a characteristic of God's sovereign will but it is not a law of his nature, for as it was observed earlier, he has no knowable nature.[28] God is not necessarily loving by nature, nor is he necessarily good, just, compassionate,

23. Cragg, *Call*, 40.

24. Ibid., 40.

25. Ibid., 40.

26. Qur'an, 85:16.

27. Rahman, *Major Themes*, 3.

28. Cragg, *Call*, 42.

kind, and holy. He may only be any number of these things because he so wills. In this way the antithesis of God's love is also seen in God's actions. He is "the One Who leads astray," "the One Who brings damage," "the Bringer-down," "the Tyrant," and "the Haughty."[29] These pejorative terms of description confirm that in the Islamic tradition God is not only without a consistent nature, he is without a nature altogether.

If any Muslim is to declare that God does indeed have a nature then a serious and obvious logical problem arises. To have a nature is to act in accordance with that nature and that nature alone. To have a nature is to be incapable of anything outside of that nature. For the Muslim, if God is to have a nature then he is to be bound to that nature as a hostage bound by chains. This hostage will then be eternally coupled to that oppressive and limiting character. For the God of Islam to be loving by nature is for him to be incapable of everything that stands in contradiction to that nature. For God to be loving by nature is for him to be incapable of acting in ill-will and discord. Yet, for the Muslim, God is quite capable of malicious and damaging tyranny, for nothing is beyond his will. With this in mind we are left either in the logical contradiction of a God with a dual nature of good and evil, or in the acknowledgement that God does not act in accordance with a divine nature, but rather in accordance with a divine will.

For the Muslim, there is nothing that God cannot be if he so wills. God does not need to love. He is not bound by love. He has no more reason to love anyone, than to hate. There is no divine standard of goodness that flows from God as from his nature. For the Muslim, altruistic concern, compassion, benevolence, and goodwill have no universal meaning. These things may be no more good than they are evil, because God himself has no nature that pronounces him any more good than he is evil.

This stands in sharp contrast to the God of Christianity. For, within the Christian tradition, God is understood to possess a nature, and this nature consists of goodness and love. This nature is not a limitation but a metaphysical necessity if God is to exist and relate to his creation. God's nature is not a constraint as is the gravity that keeps our feet planted on this earth. Since God has a nature, his actions reflect his nature, and he can therefore be known through the actions of his nature. In this regard, the God of Christianity can be trusted and worshiped since the

29. See Cragg, *Call*, 43.

followers of Christ are able to know the God to whom they direct their praise. To know God is to know that God *is* love. To know God is to know that God is by his nature loving. Having recognized the nature of divine love, Christian theologians have noted seven significant elements of this love.

God's love is *uninfluenced*. God's love is not dependent on any object or creature but, rather, is "free, spontaneous, and uncaused."[30] This is said in agreement with Francis Schaeffer's assertion that true love can only exist within the intra-Trinitarian relationship. First John 4:19 states that God loved humans before they loved him. In fact, this uninfluenced love was shown while humans were still loveless, and unwilling to respond to God's love.

In addition to the uninfluenced aspect of God's love, one might also add the *eternal* aspect. Just as God exists eternally, so also his love exists eternally. Jeremiah 31:3 speaks of the everlasting love of God. Such love does not cease to be or shift whimsically as it is said to do with Allah.

God's love is *sovereign*. Although Islam holds a similar view of God's love, the difference is that while in Islam, the natureless God chooses to act in love, the God of Christianity acts in accordance with his nature. Just as the Christian God will always exist because he cannot fail to exist, so also will he always love because he cannot fail to love. God's love is very much tied to his reign over his creation.

God is *infinite* and so, too, is his love. [31] His love knows no end. Where ever God is, there his love is also. It penetrates the deepest places, and is extended to the farthest reaches. The love of the omnipresent God is always there. His love is unfailing, and follows his beloved, piercing and infiltrating, tracking, pursuing, and reaching on and on.

God's love is *immutable*. "It knows neither change nor diminution."[32] Romans 8:35–39 declares that nothing can separate God's love from those to whom his love is directed. Those who God loves today will be loved tomorrow, for God's love never fails.

God's love is *holy*. It is set apart from the fickle and capricious love to which humans are so often subjected. The idea of holiness speaks to

30. Pink, *Attributes*, 78.

31. Though Pink states that God is infinite in regard to time, it may be better to think of God in terms of eternality. Infinity is a temporal term, but God, though he relates to a temporal universe, is himself eternal.

32. Pink, *Attributes*, 80.

perfection. In the moral sense, God is perfect in his love and loves what is good and right. There is no love of evil to be found in him. And if God's love is perfect, then there is no time when, nor place where God's love can fail. Love's perfection implies love's consistency.

God's love is *gracious*. God loved the people of the world so much that the Father gave his only begotten Son as a sacrifice for the redemption of all mankind.[33] God the Son gave his life freely in the ultimate demonstration of love to save those who deserve no better than eternal separation from the Father. In this way, God extends his love graciously to the world.[34]

It has been shown that love cannot simply be reduced to some emotive condition of a progressive humanity. As stated early on, love is not some profound and lofty emotional or cognitive state. It seems most reasonable to observe that love is there because the Trinity is there. It seems most reasonable to acknowledge that love flows into the human heart from the Lord of the universe.

For the Christian, there are some things that God is and some things he is not. He is holy, he is gracious, he is good, he is trustworthy, he is just, and he is love. But, he is not evil, nor will he act in an evil way. For the Muslim, there is nothing that God cannot be if he so wills. Like the God of Christianity he too acts in holiness, in goodness, in justice, and in love. Yet, he is mischievous, he is damaging, he is tyrannical, and he is destructive in his will. The God of Islam loves only because he wills to love. The God of Christianity loves because he is love. Tell me, from which God can love truly flow?

LOVE, FREEDOM, AND THE KNOWLEDGE OF GOD

Once again I find myself standing motionless at the diverging path in the yellow wood, as there is still one more item to consider before I choose the path of Islam or the path of Christianity. I must proceed but I am not yet entirely certain of my course. I find myself obliged to linger in this reflective disposition for a moment longer. After all, one should not act hastily in the presence of a forked path, nor should one be discouraged from further exploration. At this point I am inclined to think I know

33. John 3:16.

34. These seven descriptions of love come from Arthur W. Pink's "The attributes of God," and are a good basic overview of the Christian understanding of God's love.

which way to turn and I am eager to continue my journey. Trepidation shall not send me home for I am determined to find love's source. In peering though the mist, I can gather much about these paths and the places they might lead.

Turning home cannot be an option because as I have already seen, there is no satisfactory answer behind me. If I do not turn to go home, to sit in peace and comfort and ignorance with a nice cup of tea and warming fire, then I must choose which of the two options I will take. I must gaze on ahead and I must study the terrain one last time before determining which path will best accommodate me on my journey. Most importantly, I must decipher the end result to the best of my knowledge. I must find out where these paths lead so as not to find myself at the dismal point of a dead end. In this realm of worldview, dead ends are not clearly marked and often take the form of an intellectual precipice. I dare not cast myself into some abysmal belief of incoherence. Unlike paths of dirt and gravel, paths of reasoning and philosophical inquiry will lead to far more serious consequences. After examining each philosophical outlook I must choose that which is most intellectually sound. A path must be chosen that best corresponds to reality.

Love is the goal of this journey, and there is one final question to consider before either the God of Islam or the God of Christianity is pursued. That question is this: "What role does the relationship between human decision and divine sovereignty play in the human ability to love?" As will be seen from the answers provided by these two worldviews, the destinations provided by the divided path have little in common. Below the surface, two very different worldviews will emerge. On first glance, the Islamic and Christian views of God's divine will appear equivalent, just as a body of salt water and fresh water appear the same from the shoreline. Yet, the deeper one goes beneath the rippling water, the closer he will come to knowing the God of love.

Christian and Muslim alike affirm that God is creator, that God is sovereign, and that God in his omniscience knows every detail of the future of his creation. There is no element of creation that escapes him and there is no secret that can be kept from him. He is not taken by surprise nor is his will confounded by the craftiness of any human agent. By his will he extends love to those on whom he will have mercy and he places love in the hearts of men by his grace. Human love exerts itself under the sovereign watch of God.

In the *Hadith*, or Islamic tradition, there is a story of an argument that was ignited between two of Muhammad's followers. It is said that Abu Bakr and Umar began to dispute whether God decrees both good and evil, or only good itself. As the argument was brought to Islam's great prophet he gave a response that reveals much about who the Allah of Islam is. Mohammad answered that God decrees both. He decrees what is sweet and what is bitter; he decrees rebellion and submission alike.[35] There is an admittance of divine causation that appears in Mohammad's reply as it does also in the pages of the Qur'an. The king's decree is not made so that his subjects may then choose whether or not to obey; his decree is the actual cause of both their obedience and lack thereof. In essence, Muhammad's reply to the dispute of his followers reflects a view of God as the divine determiner of all things.

In agreement with the Hadith, the Qur'an also affirms God's absolute will in Surah 32:13, where God has said that had he so willed, he could have saved all people from Hell. God is absolute will, and he wills both good and evil, both love and hatred. So absolute is his divine will that he alone acts. In this way, for a human being to will an act is for that person to infringe upon God's divine command and authority over every action. In essence, human action is a contradiction to divine will. There is, therefore, one active agent in the universe and that is God. Everything else that exists is passive. One Muslim theologian has said that God alone is the "only one who does anything. When a man writes, it is Allah who has created in his mind the will to write. Allah at the same time gives power to write, then brings about the motion of the hand and the pen and the appearance upon paper."[36] The *Al-Nasafi Creed* states that God has created all actions of both belief and disbelief, and of obedience and rebellion. As Surah 9:51 declares, "Nothing will happen to us except that which God has decreed for us." For the Muslim, the human being is likened to a marionette, moving, speaking, loving and hating at the command of God.

In the same way such imagery would seem to be painted of divine and human interaction in Christian Scriptures. Isaiah 64:8 describes the divine relationship to man as that of a potter to clay. While such a description of God is likely to conjure up images of a capricious puppeteer bringing ruin on his morally neutral subjects, this is by no means the

35. Jeffery, *Islam*, 150.
36. Nehls, *Christians Ask*, 21.

intent of the biblical potter and clay analogy. The intent of this analogy is to declare God's complete awareness of, and interest in, his creation. It is not to show that God coerces his creation to hatred and evil. It is a declaration of God's power as creator, and God's sovereignty as sustainer.

By contrast, the God of Islam is the only mover, the only doer, the only cause of all that is. His absolute will and divine decree over all things cements his reign over every action from the greatest to the most minute and evokes three theological problems that build upon one another and that loom ominously like the shadow of a nearing storm.

Firstly, the Islamic view of God supports the idea that since God wills and decrees all things, including hatred, those who hate have done the will of God. Now, this is not a theological problem if one simply claims that God decrees to allow human hateful behavior. In this case God would decree within causing. The problem arises if it is God himself who acts in evil through a human agent. If God himself is the creator of evil then there is nothing by which the goodness and rightness of love can be gauged. Each moral act is subsequently reduced to a simple divine decision. Each act is good because it stems from God's will, and God's will is good. In this way, an act of love may be good because God ordained it to be good. Yet, an act of hatred may also be good because God ordained it as good. The Islamic view of God must allow that all things are good since all things are ordained by God. Even the vilest atrocities may be ordained as good. The torture and murder of children may be ordained as good. The destruction of innocent life may be ordained as good. Every form of hatred may be good because it is ordained by God.

This problem does not affect Christianity in the same way, because though God allows acts of violence, torture, and hatred to take place, he nowhere in Scripture confuses such acts as good. God's decrees of divine judgment against the Canaanites were not acts of genocide in which God took pleasure. These acts were, rather, the result of a divine verdict against a people of such horrific vileness and rebellion, that God saw fit to will their punishment. The Christian God wills such things in accordance with his attributes of love and justice. The Islamic God defines love and justice in accordance to his will.

Secondly, just as the God of the Qur'an ordains hatred, he also *causes* hatred. He is the author of hatred. He is the creator of evil deeds. He is the only agent in the universe that acts, and so, as the human being puts aside altruism and goodwill in favor of selfish gain and egotistical achievement at the expense of others, it is God who has acted. He causes all things to come to pass. He must, therefore, be the divine source of hatred.

Again this stands in contrast to the God of Christianity who holds human beings responsible for their own actions. It is not God who sins through human agents; it is human agents who sin and rebel of their own accord. In this way, God's judgment of the wicked can be wholly and completely just, for it is not God who coerces their depravity.

Finally, if it is God alone who acts in a completely passive universe, then there is but one agent in the universe. There is only one mind that thinks. There is only one volition that wills. Every hint of creation, whether angel, or animal, or human, is extinguished in the presence of the divine. There is nothing apart from God himself that possesses mind, will, or rationality. With this in mind, human essence is obliterated, God is reduced to a vague pantheistic deity, and love is ruined. It is made to mingle and mix with hatred until the two are indistinguishable as in the Eastern non-dualistic philosophies.

This Islamic God is either without essence or is essentially confused. Yet, if such a God wills, decrees, and moreover creates both love and hatred, then perhaps we have in fact discovered something of a nature in him. After all, can God create love and not himself be loving? Can God act malevolently and not himself be malevolent? As I consider this question my thoughts bring me to the relationship between character and action. A mirror will always reflect that which it faces. It will always reveal that which it sees. A mirror is not a window to another world. It is exactly the opposite. It shows only what appears to it. Like Dorian Grey's infamous portrait, that which is seen reflects character and character clearly depicts all of its own atrocious vulgarity.

Though both the Qur'an and the Bible speak of God as one who causes certain hateful or evil actions, these things must be understood in context. In the Qur'an God forces men to perish eternally, and he coerces unbelief.[37] In the Bible God is said to harden hearts and create disaster.[38] Though the two depictions of God seem indistinguishable, there is a difference. In the Bible, God's decrees in allowance of evil or hatred are secondary to his decrees of salvation and love, and these de-

37. Qur'an, 7:178–79; 36:7–10.
38. Exodus 9:12; Isaiah 45:7.

crees are performed in context to his nature and in light of his ultimate salvific purpose. For God to harden a heart is for him to simply allow that which is already hard to remain so. For him to decree disaster is for him to restrain any intervention in the already existing disasters of a fallen world. For the Christian God to bring destruction is for him to judge those who mock his grace and refuse his love. God may use evil to bring about a greater good but he is not the creator of evil.

In the Qur'an, God's decrees are never secondary. He causes evil or destruction as much as he causes salvation and love. He directly chooses to love some and hate others. As Surah 7:179 attests, God himself fills hell with the souls of men. In contrast, though the God of the Bible is said to have loved some and hated others, as in the case of Jacob and Esau, his love and hatred represent his choosing of one and his allowance of the other to remain in his own wretched state.[39] The God of the Bible does not create men for hell; rather, he creates hell for those who desire it.

The Christian has claimed that the particular theological and philosophical problems evident in Islam do not plague his worldview. He appeals to immunity from the disastrous implications of Islam. Yet, he too worships a sovereign and omniscient God whose divine decree rests over all creation. So what will the Christian say to the claim that the foreordination of both love and hatred usurp man's moral responsibility?

In contrast to Islam, it is said that the God of the Christian tradition is not only a God who predestines and foreknows, but a God who offers freedom to human agents. The Scriptures speak specifically of a God who foreknows those who will come to him in repentance. In this regard, it seems that what God foreknows must necessarily happen, since God's knowledge of the future locks such future events into reality as if they had already taken place. Yet Christians will also point to Genesis 3, where Adam and Eve were given a choice to either obey or give in to the temptation of recalcitrance. This test of obedience was a true probational freedom, and the failure to pass this test was the non-coerced choice of our first parents. Christianity claims that God demands love, yet allows humans to choose love. Again, God detests hatred, yet allows humans to live in hatred. Where Allah may cause evil by his will, the Trinity of Christianity will in his mysterious sovereignty *only* allow for evil as a result and consequence of human responsibility.

39. Romans 9:13.

For the Christian, humans are responsible for their actions because they possess a certain amount of freedom to act. But freedom to act and to choose are different still from complete libertarian freedom. Freedom has its limits and to these limits humans are bound. For the Christian, human freedom is limited on three levels: physical ability to act, intellectual ability to act, and spiritual ability to act.

Consider physical action. As I sit and look out my window toward the Rhone River I can see an expanse of streets and buildings that extend toward old Lyon. I can imagine the cool water of the Rhone with its swirling shades of green, grey, and blue that reflect the autumn sky. If I so chose, I could walk to the river, stoop down and touch my fingers to the water. This, I could do freely. Yet, there are things I cannot do, even in my freedom. I cannot step out on the water and walk across to the other bank. I cannot in all my freedom defy such simple laws of nature. And so in the physical realm, I lack certain freedoms.

Consider now the intellectual ability to act. I can listen to the traffic below my window. I can pull the curtains back and watch as people move about. I can hear the sounds and believe that what I have sensed is real. I can be told that it is 10:37 in the morning, and I can choose to believe this information. I can be given an argument for the validity of Buddhism and choose whether or not to accept it as true. I can choose to believe many things about reality but still I am not completely free. I cannot simply will a treasure chest of gold into the middle of the room. I cannot believe that it is as black as night outside when I know that I am sitting here in the morning light. I cannot give intellectual assent to the idea that there is a gold fish with purple spots flying in the middle of the room. I can certainly imagine such a creature, but I cannot, in all my freedom believe in my mind that such a thing exists in front of me at this very moment. It is clear that the human intellect lacks certain freedoms.

In the same way spiritual actions, and the moral choices that flow from them, have their limits. According to the Christian view of the human spiritual condition, I am a fallen man. I am a man who sins, who rebels against God, and who says and does unkind things. I have been dishonest, I have been unfair, I have hated and loathed, and I have engaged in various other forms of wickedness. With this being said, I am to be held accountable before God for my actions. I have acted in an unholy way in the presence of a God who cannot tolerate such things. Because of my free choice to sin against this holy sinless God, I am to be eternally removed from his presence. I suppose that I am to be damned without hope. Yet, if I were completely free to make choices that would affect my spiritual state, I should be able to freely fix my spiritual condition as easily as I ruined it in the first place. I should be able to roll up my sleeves, march right up to God, and say: "I have chosen to let myself into heaven like it or not." Yet, Christians will not say this. Rather, they will understand that their salvation is a gift of God's grace and not of any action that humans decide to perform on their own.[40]

For the Christian, freedom is understood in light of these limits. It is not defined by what humans can imagine but by what humans can do in consideration of the restraints that exist naturally around them. Humans are free to act in love as God extends his grace to them, and they are likewise free to hate both God and man. Whether love is chosen or rejected, the morally conscious creature will be held accountable for his choice. In rejection of Islamic fatalism, Christianity affirms that those who despise love have hung themselves on a gallows of their own making, as all humans have a moral responsibility to love and a moral responsibility to resist hatred.

While man plays a significant part in the workings of time and space, there is a God whose sovereignty extends over all his creation. Though he is sovereign, the Christian Scriptures do not teach that this God causes all human action simply by knowing what will take place.[41] We humans see dimly from our intellectual vantage point but God sees far more lucidly. Some would suggest that while humans see all things as occurring on a temporal chronological scale of past, present, and future, God sees all things as occurring in a divine sense of the present, as if looking in from outside of time. One might say that for God to know the future is not for him to know what you *will do* but for him to know what you *are doing*. From a divine perspective God *knows*, from a human perspective God also *foreknows*. The eternal God whose existence is not dependent on time and space and who is not limited by time and space looks in on and interacts with the four dimensions of time and space from within and without.

40. Ephesians 2:8–9.

41. The response to the question of divine foreknowledge and human freedom takes several forms in Christian circles. For further reading on both Reformed and Arminian views see Beibly and Eddy, *Divine Foreknowledge*. This volume offers arguments on simple foreknowledge as well as the Augustinian, open theist, and middle knowledge positions.

It is very possible that divine foreknowledge and human responsibility are quite compatible. A legitimate human choice can be made even when it appears that foreknowledge has rendered that choice beyond execution. For example, at this moment I am sitting in a room writing on paper. I could at any time leave the chair in which I sit and turn the handle of the door that leads from here to an adjacent room. I would then exit this room in favor of the other room. But I do not move. Instead I choose to stay seated here where I am. It is a legitimate choice. Now suppose that later on, when my work is finished, I attempt to leave the room. I reach for the handle of the door, but alas I find that the door is locked and I cannot exit. I now realize that though I freely chose to stay within the room I had no other alternative. I was locked in though I chose to remain.

God's foreknowledge does not necessarily coerce that which it sees. The Christian can remain true to the teachings of Scripture which have acknowledged the two important facts that, firstly, whether humans choose to love or to hate they are responsible for the consequences of such, and that, secondly, God in his eternal foreknowledge and grace has given humans the ability to respond to both him and to other human beings with love.

Both Christian and Muslim are faced with a certain level of mystery when dealing with the issue of God's will and sovereignty in context to love. If one is to make the assertion that a supreme being exists then one is left with a natural divide between the supremacy of that being and the limits of man. But as I have said before, the Christian and Muslim advance dissimilar views of God. While one of these creates love and allows evil, the other creates both. While one is loving by his very nature, the other will not have a nature. While one loved us though we hated him, the other loves only those who loved him first. Again, I ask, which of these is the God of love? With less hesitation, I am prepared to respond.

THE CALIGINOUS PATH

As I set out to discover love, I found that in spite of overbearing hatred, love exists. I found that while love exists it could not be explained by the naturalists, or the metaphysical materialists. I found that love could not be explained by the full force of all the gods of polytheism, nor by the ubiquitous god of pantheistic non-dualism. Likewise, the offer of monarchotheistic as a viable choice, proved powerless to show me something real and meaningful. As I continued my searching, I set out down the path of theism to see if love was there, and I found a fork in the road. I tested my options. I asked each path for a reason to proceed. I strained my eyes to gaze upon that which each path had to offer. One path I found to be caliginous and dark, without hope, and without clarity. The other path I found inviting. It spoke of a God who really is there, and who really does love. That path called me to an understanding of a God who loves because it is in his nature to do so. The path beckoned me to open my eyes and see the living triune God whose perfect eternal love is not dependent on man. This God is the only possible source of love, for he is by his nature loving and he has set an example of love within the hearts and minds of man by demanding that we act in love just as he loved us.

Christianity was the best explanation for love, and so I pursued it. With walking stick in hand I set out down the path to understand this love that I had seen in the Christian God. Yet even on this good path I was waylaid twice. At first I came to a seemingly impassable river. Its name was *The Hiddenness of Love*. It swept across the path like a rushing torrent begging to know why, if God is really there, love is so elusive. And when I had crossed this river I came next to a chasm that bore the name *The Prevalence of Hatred*. From the ravine a voice demanded to know why, if God is really there, hatred consumes the hearts of men. I could not wait agnostically in the face of these challenges and I could not return to my home in *Dirt Place*. The next two chapters will be dedicated to the means by which I safely crossed these final impeding obstacles.

5

The Hiddenness of Love

Love and the Human Condition

Imagine a young couple, husband and wife, who, leaving their city and country behind, set out on a journey that will take them to a more prosperous land where they will make their new home. Before the age of the automobile or the airplane, they travel largely by foot—their belongings having been placed in a small cart and pulled by a beast. Though they know their ultimate destination, the roads that lead them there are unfamiliar. They persist upon their journey for several days until they come to a mountain range with impassible gorges, and summits of unassailable height. Knowing that they will make their home on the far side of this prodigious expanse, they search for an adequate road.

It is not long before they come to a road as straight and well-groomed as any they have ever seen before. The road cuts through the mountains with not so much as even a gentle incline and passes through beautiful forests of green, laced with waterfalls and cool shade. But before they enter the forest gate, they are stopped upon the road by an old man who claims to own all the land between them and the mountains. He speaks to them for some time of the beauty of his forest, but assures them of far greater things that await them on the other side if only they are careful to remain true to the road. They will arrive unharmed and unscathed only if they forsake the beauty of the forest and cling fast to the path before them. "The forest is enchanted," he warns them, "and those who stray within its bounds are forever lost within."

With this warning in mind, and with no other option, the young couple proceeds. Among sleeping fir trees and shadows they pass, all the while enjoying the beauty of the dark wood. They laugh and talk of the life they will have in their new country as they move ever nearer their destination. But soon the cool springs and soft forest floor beckon them to stop and rest. Though the old man's warning echoes in their heads, they are soon enticed by the forests alluring charm. Before they realize it, they find themselves enjoying that fresh and supple land to its fullest. They rest beneath a tree not far from the path. They wade in the cool springs of water nearby, and they take their lunch as they sit in the soft grass. The rest they enjoy there is much needed but soon they realize that they must be on their way.

As they walk back to the path they find their belongings just as they had left them. They make ready and continue their journey, but as they advance the path narrows to a point at which it is indistinguishable from the thick forest before them. Gazing through the dark cloak of green, it is only distant blackness that meets their eyes, as the path has faded from sight. "How can this be," they think to themselves. "How could such a wide and well kept path just disappear?" With the path gone, there is no hope of continuing ahead through the hazy green. In a panic they turn to walk back toward the old man's home. They know it lies far behind them, but they have nowhere else to go. They hurry along the road but again it fades away. There is nothing, only trees. The path is lost and the forest closes in around them. Now with terror they realize their doom.

They will never leave that place. Forever they will live there in regret and anger. Their dreams of a happy home in a new and prosperous land will fade and they will forever live in shame. They will blame each other for their doom, and they will grow to despise each other as they witness the joys of youth and hope wilt away.

In many ways we humans live as those trapped in a dark wood. Our lives are anything but a fairy tale land of perfect happiness. Doom and despair seem to us at times more real than love. We want love but we fail to live by it. We desire love but instead we practice everything but love. This dreadful paradox of the love and hatred, cohabitating yet warring within my heart, leaves me unsettled. Though it has already been concluded that love does indeed exist, and though there is now some hope that love might be explained by the Christian faith, despair's oppressive yoke still rests upon my neck as I witness love's elusive flight from the heart of humanity. Just as the young couple discarded their future of promise in return for one of gloom and obscurity, so also has love been discarded and replaced with enmity and ill-will. Christianity has offered some hope of an explanation for love's existence, yet, can it explain love's elusiveness? Love seems to be no more prevalent than hatred, and these two remain in constant conflict with each other to the point where I am inclined to wonder what went wrong with this dreadful mess we call humanity.

The true religion must not only explain love's existence; it must also explain the infelicitous wrong-doing that so habitually takes place within this world. It must explain why so often love is nowhere to be seen, and why we live in this wretched paradoxical state. It must ultimately explain how love might be retrieved and enjoyed. If Christianity cannot explain love and hatred, and all the questions that surround these two, then it must be rejected. And if it is rejected then the hearts of men must be filled with despair, because no other theistic, polytheistic, pantheistic, mystic, existential, or naturalistic religion, philosophy, ideal, or superstition has yet to decipher the enigma of love.

It seems that too many have abandoned love. Men have grown so accustomed to hatred, discord, and violence that they hate even love. This has been man's response to love. Those who do not hate it, ignore it, and those who want it, can rarely find it if they try. Why is love so elusive? Where is love? Certainly it exists as has been proven both by reason and observation? But where is this Christian God who is said to distribute a vast abundance of love? Must the great storehouse remain locked? If love is divine then in what hidden realm does its pure and authentic beauty remain concealed? If indeed this Christian God is the true God of love, and if his existence alone explains the few occurrences of love for which we humans thirst, then why are there so few of these occurrences? Christians claim that God created man in his very image, yet man reflects so little of what God is said to be. Where is the proof of our glory? Where is the proof that we will reflect the love of God and his goodness? Have not the Christian Scriptures themselves declared that we humans are beings of glory and honor? If this is true, then why do we not glorify and honor love?

These desperate questions may very well be answered in the pages of Scripture, and the mysteries of love may very well be deciphered by understanding love in its relationship to human greatness and human wretchedness. These two opposing forces are both very real. After all, if human greatness was not a reality, then not only would love be impossible for humans, but so also, humans would contradict everything divine and testify by their very nature to the absence of God. Yet, if human wretchedness was not a reality, then there would be no hatred—no antithesis of love—and humans would love always and perfectly. Neither of these conditions have been obtained. Both love and its antithesis are still there and are being faithfully confirmed each and every day by human greatness and wretchedness. What can Christianity do to explain this condition?

THE BEST OF TIMES, THE WORST OF TIMES

Many will likely recall the notable opening words of Charles Dickens' novel, *A Tale of Two Cities* that begins with the brilliantly scribed monograph:

> It was the best of times, it was the worst of times, it was the age of wisdom, it was the age of foolishness, it was the epoch of belief, it was the epoch of incredulity, it was the season of light, it was the season of darkness, it was the spring of hope, it was the winter of despair, we had everything before us, we had nothing before us, we were all going direct to heaven, we were all going direct the other way.[1]

To lift this text from the pages of Dickens' novel and insert it in the pages of human existence is to describe with no greater cogency the human condition. We were filled with love, we were overflowing with hatred, we were quick to show kindness, we were encumbered by selfish lust, we were the wellhead of greatness, we were the quintessence of wretchedness. Understanding this converse human nature will help shed much luminosity on love's seldom emergence in human thought and behavior.

To know the best of humanity is to look no further than the greatness with which God is said to have made mankind. The Psalmist declares: "What is man that you are mindful of him, the son of man that you care for him? You made him a little lower than the heavenly beings and crowned him with glory and honor. You made him ruler of the works of your hands and put everything under his feet."[2] This is human greatness, to be filled with glory and honor, and given a position of au-

---

1. Dickens, *Tale of Two Cities*, 11.
2. Psalm 8:4–6.

thority over the physical universe. It is humans alone who understand the complexities of reality, and it is humans alone who realize that there are an immeasurable number of things which are quite beyond us.

This great and mighty human is able to achieve, and driven to know. Unlike the animal that merely grazes on grass for survival, the man knows *what* the grass is. He alone knows how this grass grows. He knows where it grows best. He understands its cellular structure, and its genetic makeup. He alone observes and explains the process of photosynthesis. This man alone speaks of the grass in propositions and describes it in poetic detail. He sees it and interprets it in images of sketching, painting, and sculpture. Man's greatness is seen in his capacity to discover, to invent, to create, and to understand.

Man's greatness is seen in his ability to love. It is seen in his ability to give selflessly of himself. It is seen in his ability not only to act in love but to ask himself what this thing called love even is. When he loves, his love is more than an instinct; it is connected to a mind, a consciousness. There is even something of eternity in this capacity to love. When man loves his love is good and gentle and true. It is something that seems to flow directly from the goodness of God, its eternal source.

Examples of human love so naturally point to the existence of a loving God, just as a monument points to some great and worthy deed of valor from the past that ought to be remembered. Human greatness points to something great, and human love points to a laudable and divine love. But what are we to make of human wretchedness? The same Psalmist who declared the glory of man went on to say: "The Lord looks down from heaven on the sons of men to see if there are any who understand, and any who seek God. All have turned aside, they have together become corrupt; there is no one who does good, not even one."[3]

These words were echoed many centuries later by the Apostle Paul who so aptly reminded the early Christians that:

> There is no one righteous, not even one; there is no one who understands, no one who seeks God. All have turned away, they have together become worthless; there is no one who does good, not even one. Their throats are open graves; their tongues practice deceit. The poison of vipers is on their lips. Their mouths are full of cursing and bitterness. Their feet are swift to shed blood;

3. Psalm 14:2–3.

ruin and misery mark their ways, and the way of peace they do
not know. There is no fear of God in their eyes.[4]

The Christian Scriptures make clear that apart from God's grace
there is no one good. These Scriptures make clear that apart from God's
grace the world is devoid of selfless goodwill and kindness. They make
very clear that apart from God's grace the world is truly and completely
empty of love and it effects. God's grace may very well be the means by
which love is available to us, but much like God's love, we might ask the
same question of his grace: where is it hiding?

If Christianity truly does offer the only explanation for love, then
why does God not lavish this love upon us? How can a so-called loving
God withdraw and mask his love from us? Why must he draw so dark a
curtain over it? We long for love and yet he keeps it shrouded. He allows
us to hate, and murder, and despise one another. He allows us to despise
even him. He allows our creativity to work in ways that bring on suffering, death, and ugliness. He allows us to cast away our image of goodness
and love into the mire and filth of our own making and care for nothing
more than ourselves. Is this the God we are to love? How paradoxical!
We want to love and yet we are devoid of it. We are far better at hating.
And where is God to save us from hatred? Where is his hiding place?
Must he leave us to this sinister dichotomy?

Greatness and wretchedness, this is the human enigma. Love and
hatred, this is what flows from the hearts of mankind. The proliferation
of hatred and negligence that has taken shape seems to prove that even
the Christian God is inconsistent in his dealings with man. Even he,
in all his power and goodness, seems unable or unwilling to maintain
a world of perfect love. Yet, these desperate conclusions may soon be
unmade and the devastating conflict soothed once more. Our condition
is not hopeless, and the human enigma is not left unanswerable. Let us
therefore move forward toward understanding this condition and let us
discover the hope of escape offered by God himself.

THE SINISTER DICHOTOMY

The indubitable reality of the ugly portrait of mankind that hangs before us is reason for concern. All at once the image is strikingly honest, strangely appealing, and yet perfectly grotesque enough to easily

4. Romans 3:11–18.

convince the skeptic of its absolute arresting beauty and reprehensible lewdness. The sinister dichotomy of human nature is framed and displayed for all to see. If one is to stop and gawk, or laugh at, or mock this curious and idiosyncratic display, he has done no more than ridicule himself. Human nature is, after all, laughable. Now, when I speak of human nature I am not simply referring to the fact that human beings are two-footed mammals that do not possess antlers, wings, or tales; I am referring, rather, to the rationality, the moral awareness, and the desires, fears, and interests that differentiate us from beasts. The thoughts of philosophers have varied greatly over the question of how the human nature is to be discovered and explained as each brings his questions and doubts. Certain existentialists have claimed that human nature is moldable, and that humans craft for themselves an essence and a morality as they see fit. Darwin and the naturalists defend the idea that human nature exists as a mere extension of biological progression. Hobbes has claimed that though humans have a nature, its antisocial leanings can only be subdued or held at bay by the authority of a strong governmental rule. In contrast to Hobbes, Jean-Jacques Rousseau has asserted that human nature will only be fully and overtly identified after the individual leaves behind the corruption of society. He declares that only by a return to the innocence of primitiveness and noble savagery can the human nature be known.

The questions concerning the nature of humanity are many, and their answers can only be found by considering our status as humans, along with our ontology, our unity and duality, our self-realization, our development of language systems, our social individuality and collectivism, our finitude, our volition, our physical makeup, our history, and our relationship to one another. As we humans seek to understand ourselves and all of these things that make up who we are, there is one thing that remains for certain: humans are in conflict. We are in conflict with ourselves; we are in conflict with God; and if that were not enough to destroy us, we add to conflict a conflict against conflict itself. Human nature has led to a painful and destructive condition that multiplies itself with every futile attempt to escape it.

Very few thinkers have been able to understand the human condition in such a salient and thoughtful way as seventeenth century philosopher and mathematician Blaise Pascal. Pascal's sensitivity to the intellectual and spiritual struggles of humanity rendered his treatment of such matters timely and relevant not only in Enlightenment Europe, but also in this present age. Pascal knew that greatness and wretchedness, squalor and beauty, truth and deceit, and love and hate do not discredit the reality of God, but, rather, expose a truth beyond denial. As Pascal studied the Christian Scriptures he came to realize the human paradox saying: "What sort of freak then is man! How novel, how monstrous, how chaotic, how paradoxical, how prodigious! Judge of all things, feeble earthworm, repository of truth, sink of doubt and error, glory and refuse of the universe!"[5]

How true this is! Pascal has explicated the biblical declaration of human magnificence and human misery. In his reflections on the whole of humanity in the Christian faith Pascal has illuminated an important insight about human anthropology. Pascal's conclusion was that, as Thomas Morris put it, "no secular philosophical anthropology is as adequate as a Christian anthropology for diagnosing our ills and accounting for our strengths."[6] Pascal was certain that the sinister dichotomy of greatness and wretchedness did not discredit Christianity, but rather endorsed it, for this dichotomy was elucidated within the pages of Scripture itself. Within these pages greatness and wretchedness have been fully accounted for and answered, and have been listed as the effect of *Creation* and *Fall*.

Created by a perfect God and corrupted by the folly of rebellion, humanity has plunged headlong into a pit of ruin. Before the Fall, love was uncorrupted, and we enjoyed its perfect warmth. We humans were royalty then. We were created to wear the splendor of greatness as a garment around us. We were entrusted with the great and noble responsibility of making a choice of eternal consequence: follow God, or follow self. Even this choice spoke to human greatness. After all, no other creature was given such a choice. No other creature was asked to freely love God. Human greatness was manifested in wisdom, knowledge, strength, moral consciousness, and volitional aptitude. Creation attested to greatness as the hand of God moved powerfully and beautifully over what had been made. Even over the best of his Creation we were the hallmark. The immensity of God's power and perfection was demonstrated in his creative power, as was his greatness, which he poured into the apex of his Creation: man. Within those countless years drawn back through

5. Pascal, *Pensées*, (131/434), 34.
6. Morris, *Making Sense*, 129.

time the heavens were spun together; the stars were thrust forth from that ancient source; and the heavenly bodies were stretched out in immense measure, orbiting by unseen forces in wait of God's next move. Then, by no more than a thought of his mind, he acted again and again to create and form the world, and when man finally awoke to walk the earth, there was something grand and splendid about him. This was no mere beast. This human was self-aware, and able to comprehend the deep questions of the universe. The man and woman God had made were able to ask, Why? Greatness was their destiny, and glory their end. This was Creation, but then came the Fall.

In the blink of an eye, humans saw their doom and withered into weakness. In frailty they fell; we fell. The freedom to choose became the death of man, for man chose himself above God, and God gave him over to destruction. He was not only aware of God but now aware of his doom. His power to comprehend all things good, noble, excellent, and true was joined by the curse of comprehending evil and acting upon it. This parasitical curse appeared and ugliness was joined to beauty, evil to good, and hatred to love. God's gift of a probational moral freedom to choose divine fellowship resulted in man's abrogation from royalty and separation from divine love.

The choice was given to man that he might be confirmed in his obedience to God and his love for his creator. Perfect holiness and continued fellowship with God were the ultimate goal, but when man sinned he invited wretchedness to join itself to human nature so that his posterity would suffer under the dominion of the depravity he imputed to them. The gift of choice was necessary if the sincerity of man's love for God was to be proved. Sincerity carries much weight.[7] The sincerity of man's love was to be demonstrated by his unrelenting hold on that which was good—his relationship with God. Our first parents were motivated to maintain this relationship by their love for God, which was marked by their obedience to God and by their love for each other. Before the Fall, the love of the man and woman was freely expressed, in that had they so chosen, they could have rebelled against it, as they eventually did. Choice was necessary if love was to be real. It could not be forced if its sincerity was to be upheld. A rational thinking mind was behind the choice to love God and others. Man was not simply automated, he

---

7. The sincerity of love is demanded in Romans 12:9.

was animated. He could truly love God because he could truly choose to love God.

In considering the role of choice in the act of love it is not difficult to see that a person's love is rendered legitimate, sincere, and substantial by virtue of being offered freely and without hindrance. Would any husband be filled with satisfaction or joy knowing full well that his wife loved him involuntarily like some mindless automaton? Would any wife find fulfillment in a husband who loved only by some external force that acted upon his volition? The answer must be no. The human being can find no satisfaction in marriage to a number, an idea, a plant, or a machine. Such mindless things lack the essential qualities that allow them to love in any way. Love requires something that only God and man possess. We cannot know we are loved unless the lover is able to truly love with sincerity of mind and heart. It is said in the Scriptures that with such unhindered love we once walked in fellowship with God. Love was expressed in this way until the day came when man freely chose to withdraw his love from God and plunge himself into a darkness from which he could never freely escape. The choice was made to rebel and to bring upon our race the nature of stifling villainy making all humanity a living, breathing, paradox. Again Pascal remarks:

> Is it not clear as day that man's condition is dual? The point is that if man had never been corrupt, he would, in his innocence, confidently enjoy both truth and felicity, and, if man had never been anything but corrupt, he would have no idea either of truth or bliss. But unhappy as we are (and we should be less so if there were no element of greatness in our condition) we have an idea of happiness but we cannot attain it. We perceive an image of the truth and possess nothing but falsehood, being equally incapable of absolute ignorance and certain knowledge; so obvious is it that we once enjoyed a degree of perfection from which we have fallen.[8]

Once more Pascal has spoken with precision into our nature. There had to be a consequence for choosing to disobey and reject God. If there had been no consequence then God's love would be mocked, his justice squelched, and his holiness undermined. Man would have gone on living in disobedience and hatred in the presence of a very ungodlike God. It is clear that man lives under the physical, intellectual, and spiritual conse-

8. Pascal, *Pensées*, (131/434) 35.

quences of his rebellion. Had man never been corrupted he would now have no knowledge of evil nor would he act upon it. Had man only ever been filled with intellectual refuse and corruption he would not comprehend things of goodness and purity. Yet, goodness and corruption, beauty and ugliness, love and violence, gentleness and rage, strength and weakness, power and frailty, courage, fear, knowledge, inanity, kindness, bitterness, wisdom, foolishness, clarity, ambiguity, hope, and destruction all vie to reign supreme in man and fight, twisted and mangled within his heart and upon his mind until he cries out to his Creator once again.

How difficult it is to delight in who we are when we consider our nature as humans. As Shakespeare said through the mouth of Hamlet:

> What a piece of work is a man, how noble in reason, how infinite in faculty, in form and moving how express and admirable, in action how like an angel, in apprehension how like a god—the beauty of the world, the paragon of animals! And yet, to me, what is this quintessence of dust?[9]

These words ring true for anyone willing to examine his nature for a moment. Is man, in his wretched state, any more than dirt? "For dust you are and to dust you will return," said God as he announced man's doom.[10] Man is little more than a blade of grass that springs up for a time, only to be withered away in the scorching sun.[11] Worse still than our fate is the fact that even the memory our loved ones' hold of us will be largely, if not completely, forgotten within a generation. In spite of this we trudge miserably along in our condition.

From the mind of humanity has come the power to create the beauty of Renaissance painting and the ugliness of poverty and squalor. From the hands of humanity have come the power to heal disease and craft weapons of war. From the lips of humanity have flowed beautiful notes and poems so riveting and true that they bring the listener to tears. Yet, from these same lips have come insult and abuse.

Just as the brilliance of summer gives way to the decay of autumn, so also do glory and wretchedness rage within the human heart, mind, and soul, bringing us to a winter of anguish. Where there were once flowers there is now cold rain. Where there was life, there is now a wind

---

9. Shakespeare, *Hamlet*, Scene 2, act 2, lines 301–6.

10. Genesis 3:19.

11. See Psalm 103.

of death blowing over the land. Where there was strength there is now brittle frailty crushed beneath the weight of mid-winter snow. Humans are no different. Seasons of truth, goodness, and hope, will give way to seasons of doubt, foolishness, and hatred.

What is left but to "know then, proud man, what a paradox you are to yourself. Be humble, impotent reason! Be silent, feeble nature! Learn that man infinitely transcends man, hear from your master your true condition, which is unknown to you. Listen to God."[12]

GREATNESS, WRETCHEDNESS, AND LOVE

Even a glimpse at the human condition reveals greatness and wretchedness. A glimpse at this condition attests to a humanity created for glory, and fallen to shambles. But what does this mean for love? Pascal has given the advice, "Listen to God," and if we humans take this advice and listen, what do we then hear?

Christianity has spoken of two categories: Creation and Fall. And these categories speak also to the dual nature of man. If this nature is defined by duality, then this duality carries over even to love. There is no better explanation for why we humans are capable of the most selfless acts of love, and the most heinous acts of hatred.

This anthropological argument in defense of the Christian faith clarifies the dual condition of humanity by procuring an explanation for love's existence, as well as its hiddenness. Humans are clearly great in their love and wretched in their hatred, and the worldview that best accounts for this greatness and wretchedness is the Christian faith. Christianity has pointed us to the reality of love and hatred and has explained and answered this reality through its discourse on Creation and Fall. Love is only hidden because man himself has hidden it, and love is only unveiled by the gift of God in his good pleasure. If the hiddenness of love is reason to doubt the validity of Christianity then the hiddenness of love is all the more reason to embrace it.

God can be heard, just as Pascal suggested. God has communicated this dual condition to humans, and he has illuminated the fact that because of this condition, love has suffered. Seeing now the paradox in which we live, we must ask if there is a way of escape. Can we move beyond this current state? Can we leave the anguish of *Dirt Place* behind

---

12. Pascal, *Pensées*, (131/434), 34.

us and rest in love's abounding goodness? Is there no escape from that dark enchanted wood where we find ourselves lost with no hope of ever being evacuated into the light of day?

The human situation seems altogether bleak. We have heard the tale of Creation and Fall, but what of redemption? Christians have claimed that their God has created a good world, and yet, has allowed that world to go wrong. Everything previously said regarding greatness, wretchedness, and human anthropology has only shown that the world in which we live, with all its woes and excellence, can be accounted for and explained by Christian Scripture. But why must we live in the prevalence of hatred? Why must God allow infants to be tortured and starved? Why must a loving God let people commit heinous evils toward one another? Philosophers and theologians have wrestled with the problem for ages, but is there an answer? Even if Christianity offers the only explanation for love and its hiddenness, does it offer an explanation of the evils of hatred that vie to usurp its legitimacy?

It is one thing to know that love has been made elusive by our own choice; it is another thing to know that God allows gratuitous evil. Must this evil curse us over and over again? Must we live with this suffering? Why should we live with the promise of love and yet be entangled by hatred?

I will admit that though the reason for love's hiddenness is now made clear to me, the reason for hatred's prevalence remains a mystery. It is not difficult to understand that God gave us the choice to love and hate, the difficulty is understanding why a God who claims to love us seems powerless to protect us from the cruelty of hatred. Perhaps our only hope of an explanation for love is itself a deadend. Some have said that God is powerless to prevent hatred? Some have said that he does not desires to prevent hatred? Some say he hides love from us to mock us, and ridicule us, and shame us? Some say he is an evil God who taunts us by holding out love before us like candy before a child, only to recoil it and laugh when we reach for it. Is there any legitimacy in such claims? If an escape from the land of *Dirt Place* is to be made then the problem of hatred and evil must be resolved.

6

The Prevalence of Hatred

Love and the Problem of Evil

O F ALL THOSE EVILS shoveled miserably upon humanity, whether in physical suffering or emotional pain, in the hardships of life or in lack of companionship, it is our own moral evil that batters us most thoroughly. A raging storm at sea is a dreadful matter but a mutiny is far worse. The sea does only what it is made to do. Winds move the water, churning it and making waves. Heat from the sun, evaporation, seasons, tides, and currents all have their effects bringing placid serenity or wrathful tempests. Any seasoned sailor will likely know how to interpret the signs of the sea to avoid danger and pass safely upon that prodigious mass. But when a storm takes a ship and its crew, can anyone truly blame the sea? The water is nothing more than an expanse of atoms, tossed by the wind and sloshing thoughtlessly and inanimately about. It takes no pleasure in drowning its victims, for pleasure is beyond it. It cannot be taken to court to be tried and sentenced so that justice is served against it, for it carries no guilt. Its accomplice, the wind, cannot be questioned or held until it confesses, for it has nothing to confess. A frightful gale is simply that. Mutiny, on the other hand, is another matter. When a good man is struck dead out of jealousy or hatred, and flung heartlessly into the sea by his very own crew, there is reason for greater concern. A death of this kind is no mere incident of nature, but the result of conscious moral choice. A man taken by the sea is missed and grieved, but a man taken by his fellow human beings is reason for outrage.

It is no wonder that evil carried out by one man on another is the most painful of all. We humans expect that when we place our hand in a fire it will be burned. We expect that as we grow old our bodies will fail and we will meet death. We know that in some way or another, and with varying degrees, we will suffer. But I think what hurts more than any other thing is the evil inflicted upon humanity by its own hands. The elements of nature cannot always be manipulated or resisted, and there are diseases for which we have no cure. However, when we destroy each other by our own creativity and volition, we have taken evil to a new and insidious level. We expect a certain amount of natural evil but we recoil at the savage brutality of man. It is precisely this savagery and hatred that contributes to what has come to be known as the problem of evil.

As we continue down the path of inquiry into the origin of love we come to a rotten bridge that totters precariously over the deep dark chasm of evil. If Christianity is to explain love then it also must explain hatred and the evil from which hatred springs. Its treatment of the problem must fortify the bridge enough that it might be reliably traversed.

The problem of evil has been used as an indictment against theism by philosophers from Epicurus to the abnormally obsessive anti-theistic Christopher Hitchens. From primordial to contemporary times the question has been a momentous accusation against the existence of God. After all, how can an omnibenevolent, omnipotent, and omniscient God allow so much horrendous and gratuitous evil and hatred to exist. The great skeptic, David Hume, questioned God's power and goodness saying: "Is he willing to prevent evil, but not able? Then he is impotent. Is he able, but not willing? Then he is malevolent. Is he both able and willing? Whence then is evil?"[1]

Hume has asserted that the fact of evil's existence in the world forms grounds for rejecting Christian theism. This argument from evil is considered a significant defeater of Christianity. After all the evidence for Christianity has been put in place and intellectual assent begins to give way to faith in God and in Christ, the problem of evil still hangs there like the sword of Damocles, ready to fall and strike the worldview that has thus far earned the crown of validity and coherence over all the others. C.S. Lewis affirms that if one were to follow the course on which many have been led, and becomes a Christian, that person is left with the problem of pain.[2] This problem of pain is also a problem of hatred, and ultimately, a problem of evil.

1. Hume, *Dialogues*, 63.
2. Lewis, *Problem of Pain*, 15.

Evil takes many forms as Comte-Sponville relates in his argument against the Christian God. We see it in nature, and we see it in the actions of man. For Comte-Sponville the proof against God is fortified most strongly, not by some eloquent logical argument of reason, but in the sheer length of the list of afflictions that affect the human race.[3] He speaks of plague, leprosy, cancer, Alzheimer's, autism, psychological suffering, and natural disasters as the litany grows longer and more appalling. As he examines the list before him, Comte-Sponville's logical response to all of this is simple: "C'est que Dieu n'existe pas."[4]

Comte-Sponville rightly makes a distinction between natural evils—cancer, disease, mishaps brought on by carelessness, and the elements of nature—and moral evils for which humans are responsible. Many have recognized this same distinction by classifying evils as those that result from the normal workings of nature and those that require mind. The later are the worst. Humans in all of their creativity invent ways of doing evil. They torture, they persecute, they torment others for pleasure in the most perverse and contemptible manner. In one part of the world a woman may be beaten and killed while her children watch in horror, and in another place a man may suffocate his child in its own cradle. Both natural and moral evils are horrendous to imagine and both are worthy of grief. However, the evil that I am most concerned with here is the evil defined by hatred, viciousness, and complete disregard for other human beings. It is this type of evil that stands in sharp antithesis to love.

DEAR KIND GOD

The weight of crushing hatred has been borne by many in the course of human history who falter under its subjugating tyranny and unrepentant abatement of all that is love. While many experienced sufferers have lamented the hatred of their day, I know of no other person more capable of articulating the horrors of hatred inflicted on one man by another than Fyodor Dostoevsky whose novel *The Brothers Karamazov*

3. Comte-Sponville, *L'Esprit*, 123–24. Il y a la peste, la lèpre, la paludisme, le choléra, la maladie d'Alzheimer, l'autisme, la schizophrénie, la mucoviscidose, la myopathie, la sclérose en plagues, la maladie de Charot, la chorée de Huntington . . . Il y a les tremblements de terre, les raz-de-marée, les ouragans, les sécheresses, les inondations, les éruptions volcaniques . . . Il y a le malheur des justes et la souffrance des enfants.

4. Ibid., 124.

sets Ivan the intellectual atheist in debate against his religious younger brother, Alyosha. Three scenarios, given as a discourse on hatred, from the mouth of Ivan, are worth quoting at length as he assails his brother with evidence against God. First, he speaks of the great crimes committed by the Turks and Circassians in Bulgaria brought on by the fear that the Slavs would revolt:

> They burn villages, murder, outrage women and children, they nail their prisoners by the ears to the fences, leave them so till morning, and in the morning they hang them—all sorts of things you can't imagine. People talk sometimes of bestial cruelty, but that is a great injustice and insult to the beast; a beast can never be so cruel as a man, so artistically cruel. The tiger only tears and gnaws, that's all he can do. He would never think of nailing people by the ears, even if he were able to do it. These Turks took a pleasure in torturing children, too; cutting the unborn child from the mother's womb, and tossing babies up in the air and catching them on the points of their bayonets before their mother's eyes. Doing it before their mother's eyes is what gave zest to their amusement. Here is another scene that I thought very interesting. Imagine a trembling mother with her baby in her arms, a circle of invading Turks around her. They've planned a diversion; they pet the baby, laugh to make it laugh. They succeed, the baby laughs. At that moment the Turks point a pistol four inches from the baby's face. The baby laughs with glee, holds out its little hands to the pistol, and he pulls the trigger in the baby's face and blows out its brains. Artistic, wasn't it?

Ivan continues to assail Alyosha with tales of hatred and torture, saying:

> But I've still better things about children, Alyosha. There was a little girl of five who was hated by her father and mother, most worthy and respectable people, of good education and breeding . . . This poor child of five was subjected to every kind of torture by those cultivated parents. They beat her, thrashed her, kicked her for no reason till her body was one bruise. Then, they went to greater refinements of cruelty—shut her up all night in the cold and frost of a privy, and because she didn't ask to be taken up at night (as though a child of five sleeping its angelic, sound sleep could be trained to wake and ask), they smeared her face and filled her mouth with excrement, and it was her mother, her mother did this. And that mother could sleep, hearing the poor child's groans! Can you understand why a little creature, who can't even

understand what's been done to her, should beat her little aching heart with her tiny fist in the dark and the cold, and weep her meek unresentful tears to dear, kind God to protect her?

This story of cruelty and hatred is followed by one last account from the antiquities of Russia. Here a retired general lives in luxury on a great estate. He domineers over his surfs as a king with absolute power:

> He has kennels of hundreds of hounds and nearly a hundred dog-boys—all mounted, and in uniform. One day a surf boy, a little child of eight, threw a stone in play and hurt the paw of the general's favorite hound. "Why is my favorite hound lame?" He is told that the boy threw a stone that hurt the dog's paw. "So you did it." The general looked the child up and down. "Take him." He was taken—taken from his mother and kept shut up all night. Early that morning the general comes out on horseback, with the hounds, his dependents, dog-boys, and huntsmen, all mounted around him in full hunting parade. The servants are summoned for their edification, and in front of them all stands the mother of the child. The child is brought from the lock-up. It's a gloomy, cold, foggy autumn day, a capital day for hunting. The general orders the child to be undressed; the child is stripped naked. He shivers, numb with terror, not daring to cry . . . "Make him run," commands the general. "Run! run!" shout the dog-boys. The boy runs . . . "At him!" yells the general, and sets the whole pack of hounds on the child. The hounds catch him, and tear him to pieces before his mother's eyes![5]

Things of this nature happen more than frequently in our world. And where is God when these things happen? Where is this famous God of love when evildoers succeed at iniquity and vice while the innocent suffer? The evils spoken of by Dostoevsky in his stories were evils carried out against the most innocent children. Hatred was wrapped up in those evils, festering in the deep and dark places of the mind and heart. Such evil is not simply the stuff of fiction. An asphyxiating vapor of malevolence lingers throughout the world, and knowing this I must ask again, "where is God?"

How do we even begin to answer this question? Are we left with some kind of cosmic dualism in which the all-powerful God is pitted against the all-powerful devil? "Every sweet has its sour; every evil its

---

5. Dostoevsky, *Brother's Karamazov*, 221–25.

good," said Emerson.[6] Perhaps there is some shaving of accuracy in this statement, though I doubt that the moral constitution of the universe can ever be reduced to a cosmic balance so long as it is granted that there is a good and omnipotent God. What then? Are we left with a cosmic monism, where all things good and evil flow from the same divine being? Neither of these images describe the God of Christianity. Neither of these images accurately portray the reality in which we live. For the moral evils of this world there are several more adequate rebuttals.

MYSTERY AND THE GREATER GOOD

A man's epistemic vantage point plays an enormous role in what he ultimately perceives and takes as knowledge. All I mean by this is that when a man looks at a wall he sees only what is apparent to him. He does not see the things one might imagine to exist behind the shield of timbers and concrete. He knows nothing of what lives on the other side, if at all anything lives there. His knowledge is restricted to what he perceives. From our limited epistemic vantage point we humans often fail to see the reasons behind the evils in this world. God permits evil and unbeknownst to us, he may very well have a perfectly legitimate reason for doing so. We humans look in upon only some small piece of the picture. It is as if we have stepped close to a painting with our noses touching the canvass. What do we see? A blur of color? A dark spot with light drifting in from the edges? Whatever it is we see, we lack the sight to experience the beauty of the image in its entirety. It is as if we have heard only a few measures of a symphony arranged randomly with no order. What we hear are seemingly disjointed chords. We hear the squawks and squeak, and noisy cranky displays. But when each piece is placed back into its rightful place the music takes form and we hear beauty.

Of course, there is much truth in this argument. God declares that his thoughts are higher than the thoughts of man, and that his ways are incomprehensible to mere humans.[7] There are certainly elements of love and evil that will never be understood by man, and there are always unfathomable mysteries that will limit our understanding. Who are we to think that we can read the mind of God? If it is God who formed the

6. From the essay *Compensation*.

7. Isaiah 55:8–9.

world then he is Lord over it. If it is God who gave us life then it is he who knows us better then we know ourselves.

On some level we must cry, "mystery!" But we must not do so carelessly, nor should we do so not having fully examined the problem. To haphazardly cry mystery in the face of the problem of evil is to ignore a poison as it eats away at the very one who suffers under its curse. What we do not understand will still hurt us. We cannot make it go away but we can at least prepare our hearts and minds for its assault. Admitting our ignorance of the problem of evil is only natural given that we are indeed ignorant at some level. While mystery, as a response, does not do intellectual justice to a problem that poses such a magnificent threat to Christian theism, it does have its time and place.

It must be understood that I in no way intend to bleakly gloss over the beauty and necessity of mystery. There are numerous mysteries in this universe and there is something wonderfully mysterious of God. There are hidden things of reality that finite human beings cannot and will not understand. To evoke mystery in the face of a true and real mystery makes reasonable sense, but to evoke mystery in the face of every difficulty that crosses our path is to deny our God-given minds and run from the intellectual challenges we face. To carelessly evoke mystery in the face of evil is to move on with a troubled conscience and ignore the pain of those who suffer a life devoid of love. Yes, at some point we must claim mystery and even savor that mystery, but only after we have exhausted our understanding of this Christian God and his relationship to humanity.

The relationship between God and humanity is one of love, of freedom, and of sovereignty. As sovereign, God may allow some evil things that he sees fit to pass within his divine plan, in order to achieve his will. Within the mysterious workings of God's sovereign will, it may be that God has permitted a certain amount of evil so that through suffering humans can achieve an advantageous spiritual outcome. The Christian scriptures themselves state that the trials of evil bring on perseverance that will ultimately lead to the strengthening of faith.[8] This reasoning contains much that is true. Perhaps God must allow for the potential of evil so that humans might freely choose to love and worship him, and thus have peace and joy in their relationship with him. The natural evil of a hurricane or earthquake will often bring together the people of the

8. James 1:2–4.

affected community. The challenges of poverty or need can spur generosity. The victims of a crime might respond with forgiveness. Difficulties can lead to greater joy and to more love as if there were some strange and intimate relationship between the two. This is not to say, of course, that good and evil unfold like the seasons of nature in desperate need of one another, but it does draw out the fact that good does not cease to respond to the evils of this world.

Though God may allow some evil in order to grow human character, he may also allow certain evils in order to prevent others. By allowing one evil ten others might be avoided. By allowing one act of hatred much love might later be enjoyed. In essence, the presence of some evil may bring a greater goodness and love in the end. This one evil may have the effect of causing greater good and preventing further harm. The death of some few brave social reformers at the hands of an oppressive government might prompt the activism of many more who will make a great and constructive transformation in society—a transformation that will ultimately lead to greater love, respect and prosperity.

Other examples of greater good are surveyed in the study of ethics. One such example is articulated in the problem of the corpulent fellow. In this case a man of copious structural ratios is lodged in the entrance of a cave while exploring near the seaside. Behind him are dozens of his friends, and behind them is a quickly rising tide. There is no way out but the door which is blocked up by the mass of the fat man. They push and they pull but it is no use. He will not be dislodged. Then one of the men pulls from his sack a stick of dynamite (that he just happened to have included in his provisions for the day), and as you can imagine the group returns home one fewer in number. The death of one prevented the death of many. It was Sophocles who long ago asserted that "the end excuses any evil."[9] This utilitarian utterance may be better known by the statement: "the end justifies the means."

But placing this arguably humorous story aside, why must there be even one death? Could not God have prevented even one act of evil? Even one death, one loss, one hurt, and one moment of suffering is one too many. Why must there be any evil? Why must there be any hatred? In considering again Dostoyevsky's example, did the little girl, despised by her parents, need some divine lesson in suffering so that her prayers would be substantiated and her reception of grace legitimate?

9. From the play *Electra*, 409 B.C.

Perhaps it is true that one evil prevents another. Perhaps it is true that suffering builds character and leads us to greater sympathy for others. Perhaps God does use evil to bring about greater good. But even this answer does little to alleviate the intellectual problem that remains. Others have responded to the problem of evil by suggesting that without evil man would be unable to appreciate all the good and love in the world. The difficult times lead to a greater appreciation of the good times. Candy tastes sweeter to one used to eating only cabbage. The greatest sinner experiences the greatest joy in grace and forgiveness. The difficulties of toil produce the greatest appreciation for the fruit of one's labor.

Can it truly be that God has allowed evil as a means of preparing humanity for good? Can it be that joy is sweeter after pain and love truer after an experience of hatred? One may very well answer in the affirmative knowing that context can greatly affect the results of how an experience is perceived. Simple comfort is likened to lavish indulgence for those who have never known it. One might rejoice in love after he has lived long without it. The toil and pain of a grueling foot race brings great delight when the end is reached and there is nothing left but to bask in the grandeur of victory.

There is joy in victory but bitterness in the defeat that comes more readily. What of those who never finish the race? What of those who live a lifetime without love? What of those who never know anything but difficulty? To say that one is refined by the experience of hatred and pain can be insensitive and unfair to those who suffer the horrendous hatred and evil that are so commonplace in the world. Even if evil helps us better appreciate love, why must God allow for so much of it and so often? Certainly there are other ways to grow in appreciation for love and goodness. Why must people experience physical, emotional, and spiritual evil at all? Is there no other way for us to understand the joy of goodness and love? Why does it have to be so real? Why can we not simply see visions of evil and dream dreams? Would not even a simple dream of hatred or evil help us grow to better value love? If this were so, we would wake in the morning to a world without suffering, and live only with a memory of the nightmare that troubled our slumber. We would take comfort knowing that such a place of suffering is no reality at all. Yet evil persists and drives us all the more in our search for love and goodness.

My hope is that all that has been said thus far on the subject of evil may allow for our perspective to be broadened so that we are not tempted to think that there can be no greater or better reason behind hatred and suffering. The responses above are intended to soften evil's blow, but while they may do so to some extent, they do not fully respond to the reality of the depths of the horrors of hatred.

THE BEST POSSIBLE WORLD

If one is to speak of things that are agreeable, attractive, or lovely, he is to speak in terms of the good that such things generate. People, places, objects, and ideas are often evaluated by their level of goodness or lack thereof. When goodness is applied to the spiritual realm it is seen as one of the defining characteristics of the Christian God. It is this very goodness that Christians find attractive. One need not read far into the pages of Scripture to find reference to God's goodness, a goodness that is said to be among his unfailing attributes. The opening words of the first biblical book speak of a God whose creative act was said to be good. This act of creation was good because it was performed by a good God, for his pleasure. The intrinsic goodness of the creative act was validated all the more when God himself recognized and acknowledged that goodness. This makes perfect sense, for if God himself is said to be good, then naturally, that which he made by his own good creativity would also be good and would remain good under his dominion.

When one considers the goodness of the world as described in the biblical account of Creation, it is easy to forget that this very goodness extends far beyond any specific point in linear history. An omniscient God would not create the beginning without knowing the end, and he would not make a world if he did not think it the best world of all the imaginable worlds he could have created. The good of the world was not limited to an initial creative act, but was extended through the far reaches of history and into the future to contain the tremendous excellence of the atoning cross of Christ and the beauty of an eternal kingdom where the repugnant jaws of death will one day cease to spew their insalubrious fume of hatred upon the work of God's hand. This best of all possible worlds is precisely that, because it is created by God, sustained by God, and loved by God. It is a world where man was entrusted with the responsibility to make a moral choice; and it is a world where the consequences of the choice are remedied by God himself.

God has created a world where he knows all ends, and where he allows humans a certain level of responsibility for their actions. Moreover, he has foreordained the cross of Christ as the ultimate defeat of evil and the ultimate reconciliation of rebellious man and gracious Creator. I repeat myself here only to reiterate the important fact of the goodness or *bestness* of this world from a biblical standpoint. By *bestness* I mean that of all the realities that an omniscient God could have conceived, he conceived this one, made it a reality, and declared it good. In essence, God has created the best possible world.

Some may fail to grasp the full extent of the goodness of this world as it pertains to moral freedom and to the cross of Christ in Scripture. As discussed in the last chapter, these two themes are tied to two very important Christian doctrines—the doctrines of human sin and redemption. If there was no test of human free will through the choice of obedience that God offered our first parents, could there have been a true humanity? Had humans not fallen into sin, would we have ever known the true depths of God's love when he sent the Son to the cross in our place? Scripture claims that the events surrounding the incarnation of Christ are the most important events in the history of the world. The unfathomable horror of man's rejection of God was atoned by the immeasurable riches of God's love on the cross. It is for this reason that the Christian has assurance of the *bestness* of this world.

It is worth noting here that the discussion of this world as the best possible world is not new to philosophy or theology. Such discussion has been used as a response to the problem of evil and has been discussed in various forms by numerous philosophers. In fact, the discussion of possible worlds is based on theological insights that span from medieval Catholic monks to Enlightenment philosophers and beyond. A complete philosophical analysis of possible worlds is not called for here, but I will present several steps that lead to the conclusion that this hate filled world is overshadowed by a world in which a loving God has established his authority and power.[10]

To accept the *bestness* of this world among all possible worlds it is necessary to begin with what theologians call the *aseity* of God. Aseity refers to the idea that God is a necessary condition for the existence of any possible world. A world in which God is present is not only infinitely

10. For a more complete assessment of possible worlds and the problem of evil see Gottfried Wilhelm Liebniz, *Theodicy*.

more precious than a world in which God is not present, but a world in which God is present is a logical necessity. Alvin Plantinga states that "according to the traditional doctrine of God's necessary existence . . . God is both concrete and necessarily existent, and the only being who displays both these characteristics. If this doctrine is correct, then there are not any worlds in which God does not exist."[11] Aseity is essential to who God is. He is self existing. He is necessary. If there is God, then there are only possible worlds in which he exists. An existing God cannot and would not create a universe without himself. To do this he would have to stop existing. Every world that could possibly exist, exists with God.

The *bestness* of this world stems not only from the idea that God is a necessary condition for its existence, but from the idea that a perfect God would not have created anything less than what he deemed best. In other words, for a perfect and good God, the best possible world is in fact, the only possible world. Of course, it should be granted that of what philosophers speak when they discuss possible worlds is the idea that an all-knowing God can know or imagine an infinite number of potential scenarios for the world since his knowledge is infinite. As Plantinga suggests a possible world is a reality that would exist only in the mind of God until the time he chose to actualize it, that is, if he chose to actualize it. Until that time it remains unknown and unexperienced by anyone but God himself. Granted that possible worlds exist in God's mind, I suppose that God could imagine a world exactly like this one with the exception that I have one less hair on my head. He could image a world in which I do not exist, or in which you do not exist, or in which no one exists. He could imagine a world in which everything edible tastes like pine needles. He could imagine anything and everything, but given that the omniscient God could imagine an infinite number of possible worlds, it is rather useless to think that this God would actualize or create anything less than the best of these.

Though the discussion of possible worlds can lead one to the realm of modal logic and beyond, the main principle to retain here is the fact that God is capable of imagining a great number of possible realities, that his own existence is central to any of those realities, and that the only reality with which we need concern ourselves is the one in which we live. The point that Plantinga and other philosophers make is that this world—the world you see from your window, and the world into

11. Plantinga, "Supralapsarianism," 7.

which you were born—is the best possible world. Plantinga states that "God not only has created a world that is very good, but there are not any conditions under which he would have created a world that is less than very good. It is not possible that he create such a world; every possible world in which God creates is very good."[12] This best possible world that God has made is a world that contains an overwhelming good. This is a world that expresses optimum beauty and creativity. It is a world whose simplicity, complexity, design, subtle delicacy, expression, grace, and rational form, all declare the reality of the God who is there.

In God's sovereign knowledge and supreme wisdom this is the world he thought best to create. The fact of God's goodness is itself a theodicy, or defense of the goodness and love of God in the face of evil's challenge. I dare claim that this depraved and hate filled sewer is the best possible world, and I do so by acknowledging the existence of two particularly good features: the enormously good feature of freedom and responsibility that Adam and Eve are said to have enjoyed in the Garden of Eden (which led to the introduction of evil into the world), and the enormously good feature of the redemption from evil that Christ bought about on the cross.[13]

It has been argued that this best possible world contains a certain level of moral freedom that has led to a great deal of moral depravity. But it has also been argued that this best possible world contains the incarnation, the cross of Christ, and thus, the atonement and future elimination of evil. The sum of these features confirms the veritable *bestness* of this world, where in spite of our continual rebellion against all that is good, love is made possible by God's grace. Far too often we forget this grace and blame the very God who holds evil in check. If we are to imagine a world created and then abandoned by God, how much more severe would evil become. Such a world would putrefy under the dominion of man as all that is good is siphoned from us and extinguished by our own creative devices. We deceive ourselves if we think ourselves better than this.

By acknowledging the excellence of the existence of human moral responsibility and the overwhelming good of Christ's atoning sacrifice,

12. Ibid., 8.

13. What I have said here is based upon, but not identical to Plantinga's response to the problem of evil. Plantinga's response is much more sophisticated than can be presented here and can be found in its entirety in "Supralapsarianism."

the Christian has offered reconciliation of the opposing realities of God's goodness and an evil world. He has offered hope of escape from the squalor of *Dirt Place* through the eternal love of God. It was in love that he created, in love that he redeemed, and in love that he will sustain this world. The *bestness* of this world is a thought worth our consideration in spite of the evils we face. More than a deceptive emotional state or rose-tinted lens, this *bestness* is a reality of our past, present, and future.

Does this explanation ease and comfort the minds of those who have endured past sufferings, or who remain in a state of grief even now? Does such a response eliminate the scars of hatred that cannot be hidden? Does this construal of the philosopher's mind disentangle the brambles of enmity suffered at the hands of others? Perhaps it does not. Perhaps it does nothing else but reminds us that we ourselves are the ones who murder and hate, who torture and despise, and who corrupt and damage. It is not God, but we, who have done this.

Evil done by our own hands is that which separates us from God. It is this evil that dooms us. Hatred seethes out from us, raging against both God and man, and looming as a shadow over us. We must live with the consequences of our actions. God must not be expected to simply and immediately mend every misdeed and set straight every crooked path we produce. It is not for him to undo all wrongs that have been done, but to offer healing from those wrongs. We live in a world sustained by God's love where we may come to know the gravity of our sin and the splendor of God's forgiveness.

Having explored several answers to the problem of evil there is still one rejoinder that waits to be employed, and that speaks more specifically to the definition of hatred. We have asked the questions that have led us to a definition of love, and now we must ask these questions of love's antithesis, hatred. Knowing that love proves God's existence, and knowing that hatred seems to disprove it, there is one more approach that can be taken to the problem of evil that will allow love and hatred to be understood in greater clarity. Though thoughts of the horrors of hatred do not merit the consumption of even the slightest moment of cognitive exertion, we must still force ourselves to ask the questions that will ultimately free our minds from the confusion of this enigma. And so we shall trudge along in our contemplation of this problem that plagues the theist and brings any thinker to recoil at the disgusting spectacles of hatred and evil carried out by one human on another.

THE EXTINGUISHMENT OF HATRED

Though we have explored the problem of moral evil and its effects, we have yet to delve through the strata of all that is evil in order to arrive at its foundation. As evil is defined, my desire is to understand it in perhaps a more ontological sense. Is evil an actual and accessible thing? What is the substance of evil? Is it a self-sustaining infinitely existing cosmic force? Questions such as these have been inherited by Christian thinkers of every generation and have been answered with varying degrees of success and clarity. St. Augustine was among the first Christians to explore the problem of evil, and in doing so he claimed that evil is nothing more than the privation of good. What he meant was that evil had no moral substance of its own but came about wherever the moral substance of good was lacking. Augustine's deliberations on the subject remain important even to this day as they offer some context for understanding evil and defining hatred.

Augustine's philosophical theology was largely composed in the fifth century A.D. when the Roman Empire was still hanging on to life and scholars had a keen attachment to the Greek philosophical thought that flourished into the Middle Ages. Much of this thought found its origins in Plato and in the neoplatonism of Plotinus. This is worth mentioning because Augustine's understanding of evil was largely tied to the Greek understanding of something called *forms*. These, so-called *forms*, were the highest and most real of reality. As Arthur Holmes relates in regard to the Greek understanding of form, "everything that exists, both corporeal and incorporeal, has form, and form is good."[14] Form is the ideal or the purest and truest image, while all other things are but a reflection. The physical reality of a horse is a reflection of the form "horseness." The physical reality of a cabbage is a reflection of the form "cabbageness." All physical reality reflects the goodness of form, and since this ideal is always good, then evil cannot pollute it. If evil is to pollute anything, it is to pollute only the shadow, or physical reality. In essence, evil has no form of its own, but it does corrupt that which reflects form.

I can go no further here until it is acknowledged that, though there are some important ideas to glean from Plato, ultimately Platonic and Neo-Platonic form theory stands in serious contradiction to the Christian worldview. While this Greek thinking held that the physical world is less real than the ideal world of form, the Christian holds that

14. Holmes, *Fact, Value, God*, 49.

both the physical and the spiritual worlds are of great value because every created thing has been declared good by the Creator. In a similar way, Greek thought is not well suited to imagining God as a triune and eternal deity who lovingly cares for the matter (both sentient and nonsentient) that he has created. This unsuitability of Greek thought also extends to the Christian idea that evil is a very genuine reality that menaces and corrupts a very real universe. However, in more or less agreement with at least one aspect of Platonic form theory, Christianity holds that the good derives from something otherworldly. Like any Christian would, Augustine held that the good derives from God.

Though there is both agreement and disagreement between the Platonic and Christian understanding of evil, Augustine's Platonic influence has brought some useful insight to the understanding of evil as a privation of good. The significance here is the idea that evil cannot exist apart from good.

As a prerequisite for grasping the idea of privation, philosophers have offered the analogy of light and darkness. When one reflects on the existence of light and darkness he will make several basic observations and among these is the most obvious observation that light exists. Light is a real phenomenon, exhibiting the qualities of both a wave and a particle. Though I am in no way eligible to discuss quantum mechanics, wave-particle duality, or dark matter to any further extent, I will say that on an observable level, light illuminates and creates a context by which to understand the objects around us. As the light is dimmed or removed little by little, the human eye can begin to understand what darkness means. Eventually when all light is removed, we are left with nothing. The substance of light has been removed. There is no visual reality left to contemplate. One does not see darkness, rather, in darkness one simply does not see.

To put it another way, the darkness we experience is what is left when there is no light. Darkness depends completely on light. If humans never had light of any kind and they were asked what they see, they would be dumbfounded by the absurdity of the question, because they would not even know what could possibly be meant by the word *see*. However, if they had been regularly exposed to the luminosity of daylight, and they were suddenly plunged into darkness, they would be able to describe that darkness and long once more for their sight. In the same way, those who know only hatred cannot understand love. It would confuse and confound them. However, those who know love would greatly suffer under the pain brought on by being plunged into hatred.

There are those who will deny the above analogy, by counter-arguing that hatred can self-exist, being in no way attached to love. They will claim that evil is not necessarily dependent on good. They will say that comparing darkness to evil is to drag a metaphor far too far, and falsely attempt to infer a moral assertion from a scientific one. Yes, there is some truth here as analogy only serves to clarify propositional truth and not replace it. But the truth of the matter is that absolute evil cannot exist. Even at best it is self-destructive. It would annihilate itself. It would tear itself apart and collapse at its very core. Evil cannot construct or assemble anything. It can only spoil that which already is. It can only feed on creativity, and insight, and knowledge, and virtue as a corrosive acid that twists and belies.

Evil and the hatred that stems from it could not survive if not for the life they siphon from love. Even the Greeks have said that, "absolute evil cannot exist, for to lack good altogether it would have to lack form and could therefore not exist."[15] Love creates, where evil spoils; love constructs where evil destroys. The importance of Augustine's reflections is in the fact that evil can serve as no more than a privation.

Having granted Augustine's observations and having defined love as *a gift of genuine benevolence and of merciful goodwill, passionately displayed, and emanating from an altruistic concern*, we are led to define hatred as a frustration and lack of these things. As a lack of love, hatred must be defined as *a menacing insincerity and deceptive malevolent ill-will that emanates from a complete selfishness and lack of concern for others.* Any number of further pejorative words might be added to this definition, but in any case we have an obvious divergence. Based on these divergent definitions, two arguments can be formed, one in defense of God, and one in denial of God. Both are equally valid arguments that take up arms to wage their war and prove their point. One proves God and the other disproves him. The first argument is presented in the following propositions:

(A)   Love exists,

(B)   The existence of love is explained by the existence of God,

(C)   Therefore, God exists.

15. Holmes, *Fact, Value, God,* 49.

The statements of this simple argument have been gathered only after discussing what love is and eliminating every philosophical outlook and worldview that fails to explain it. Both ethical and psychological egoism fail to devalue love. Neither the non-theistic beliefs of naturalism, nor the hyper-theistic beliefs of pantheism can explain love. Polytheism in its various forms has failed to give love credence. It is Christianity alone that has granted us any valid reason to believe in and explain love. It is Christianity alone that has offered us a drink from this sapid ambrosial cup. Yet, as we look around at the prevalence of evil in the world another set of propositions emerges that stands in contrast to everything that has been verified, forming the core of the argument against God. This set of proposition sweeps in and ruins the whole of the previous argument in three malefic strokes:

(X)   Hatred exists,

(Y)   The existence of hatred negates the possibility of a loving, powerful, and all-knowing God,

(Z)   Therefore, God does not exist.

Everything proved by love is destroyed in this argument. The existence of hatred cannot be denied, nor can the results of that hatred. What this argument tells us is that where hatred is, a loving God cannot be.

These completely opposing arguments with their opposing conclusions cannot both be true. The Christian settles on the first argument while granting evil, the skeptic settles on the second argument while granting good, and in doing so, both are at an impasse. Both of these arguments cannot be equally or viably true, and both cannot be equally or viably accepted. This is where Augustine's simple observation comes once again into play, for in light of his demonstration that hatred depends on love one can show that the argument from hatred contains a fatal weakness. If hatred is a privation of love, then one more proposition is truly needed:

(G)   Proposition (X) is dependent on proposition (A).

In other words, the existence of hatred owes itself to love. Remember that good was there first and that evil is a privation or lack of good. Hatred cannot be unless love is. This is significant because it leads to one more proposition that will bring closure to the dialectic between love and hatred and bring about a synthesis that will lay bare the hopelessness and despair of the argument from evil. Since proposition (G) shows hatred's dependence on love's existence, it is worth noting that all of the statements that flow from proposition (X) are dependant also on love's existence. Consider one further statement in which the answer to the problem finally manifests itself:

(H)   The propositions (X), and (Y), and conclusion (Z) are dependent on proposition (A).

In other words, since hatred is a privation of love and love's existence is dependent on God's existence, then hatred itself can only exist if there is a loving God as the source of all moral categories. The existence of evil does not disprove God's existence but rather confirms that there is a God who created human beings to exercise the freedom to love him. With that freedom came the potential for evil, and ultimately, actual evil. It must not be mistakenly believed that evil flows directly from God. Rather, evil and hatred come as a result of the absence of love. Hatred arises when man chooses to rejects the love that originates in God. Hatred flows from lack of concern for others, which is the privation and void of love. Hatred does not disprove God. All that hatred can do is to prove love's existence.

Within God's sovereign reign over humanity, humans are still responsible for their rebellion against God that ushered in the presence of evil in the world. The Christian Creation story relates that the fall of man came by his own seditious choice to revolt. He picked the fruit that he had been instructed not to pick. Though there was nothing particularly evil or bad about that fruit itself, it was the act of disobedience that bought evil into the world. By sinning, man gave up his freedom to love God. We, the human race, are now doomed to live in evil and hatred.

We may be doomed to evil and prone to hatred but how can this be if we were created in God's image and pronounced *very good*? Philosopher William A. Dembski asks, "How, then, could a good will turn against God? . . . Certainly freedom of the will contains in it the logical possibility of a will turning against God. But why should a good will created by a good God exercise its freedom in that way?"[16] Though Dembski acknowledges that we can do little to offer a final answer to that question he does acknowledge that "because a created will belongs to a creature, that creature, if sufficiently reflective, can reflect on its creaturehood and

---

16. Dembski, *End of Christianity*, 27.

realize that it is not God."[17] Realizing that it is not God, and yet wanting to be God, the creature can turn on God and in doing so, sin against him. This is precisely what Adam and Eve did in the garden when they invited evil into God's Creation.

The so-called moral freedom we think we now enjoy is the result of a curse. To think our rebellion somehow surprised God is folly, and to think we now enjoy complete moral knowledge and freedom is wishful thinking. Because of our rebellion we are not free but, rather, bound to sin. It is only by God's grace that we can act in love. We are slaves to our condition.

But is there no hope? The biblical book of Job relates the story of a man who lived a life of complete righteousness and goodness. He was blessed in every way, until that day that God allowed him to face suffering. In a moment's time, he lost every physical possession he owned. His wealth was carried away by his neighbors and his servants were put to death. His children were crushed to death in their home as it toppled in the wind. Everything he had was gone, but as he sat in the ashes of mourning and wept his tears of grief, he was still able to utter the words, "may the name of the Lord be praised."[18] Even as Job realized the hatred of his neighbors who stole his wealth, and even as he experienced the evil of death, he knew the reality of the fallen world in which he lived and he was able to praise his God, the creator of all that is good.

Even the best theodicies may fall short of elucidating the mystery of the reality of a perfect God in a less than perfect universe, but who is man to think he can know the mind of God. God himself has asked us, "Where were you when I laid the earth's foundation? Tell me if you understand."[19] Job knew that the evils he had experienced did nothing to disprove God's existence. On the contrary, had there been no God, Job would not even have had the moral sensibilities to acknowledge that any evils had been committed against him.

To say that God does not exist because evil exists is to acknowledge on a most obvious level that evil exists; to say that evil exists is to acknowledge there is something harmful, distressing, and unjust about evil. But then, from where did this sense of justice come in the first place? A thing can only truly be harmful, distressing, and unjust if we possess

17. Ibid., 27.
18. Job 1:21.
19. Job 38:4.

the moral ability to judge these things as such. If God does not exist then the words *good* and *evil* should be stricken from our vocabulary and replaced with a void. If nature is to replace God as the driving force of life, then we must no longer be alarmed at the reality of injury, oppression, and violence. If God is removed then there is no good or evil, only normativeness. Tim Keller has commented that "if you are sure that this natural world is unjust and filled with evil, you are assuming the reality of some extra-natural (or supernatural) standard by which to make your judgment."[20]

To acknowledge that there is evil and to recoil at the prevalence of hatred in disgust is to prove that there is something significant about our moral understanding, something much beyond us. To admit to the injustice of evil is to admit to the existence of a divine judge. Comte-Sponville has claimed that the problem of evil is the oldest, strongest and most common argument against God's existence, but I would like to suggest that it should be, rather, an argument for God's existence.

God has allowed evil and hatred to corrupt this world, but to suggest that God himself is powerless and corrupt is to fail to see his overwhelming love displayed on the cross where Jesus suffered beyond anything we humans have ever known, not merely physically, but spiritually, as he was torn from God the Father in cosmic rejection. This abandonment was made all the more painful in that it was not his own sin that brought about the cross, but all the evils of man throughout the ages.

When I am privileged with an opportunity to stroll through any of the great art galleries of the world I am often reminded of the tragic beauty in which suffering is depicted in painting and sculpture. Standing before Théodore Gericault's "The Raft of the Medusa" in the Musée du Louvre in Paris is a horrifying experience. In the aftermath of a shipwreck we find a dilapidated and makeshift raft filled to overflowing with the skeletal, cadaverous remains of a crew abandoned by their captain. Plague, pestilence, cannibalism, and madness drain the life out of each as the viewer looks on in hopeless despair. It is a reminder of the tragedy of evil, but it also shows the sliver of hope in the form of a recue ship on the far horizon. Evil and hatred are not the end of all things. There is still hope and goodness in life to remind the sufferer that life is not overwhelmingly tragic. The excellence of forgiveness, mercy, and kindness cannot be ignored. There is much that is sweet, and pure, and noble, and

20. Keller, *Reason for God*, 26.

true in the world. There is still laughter and hope. There is still gentleness and beauty. There is still overwhelming goodness in life.

Christians claim that the God of love has a plan for evil, suffering and hatred. We are assured that it will not always be this way. We will not always be plagued with evil, and even when all hope seems lost, God will bring the demise of hatred. There will be no victory for evil. The Christian Scriptures assure that the God of love will overcome and "wipe every tear" from the eyes of the redeemed. [21] There will be no more suffering, no more death, and no more hatred. All those little children killed and tortured to death will one day be held in the arms of the God of love. Those who suffer the evils of hatred and who cry out to the God of mercy will be saved. There is no doubt that love is there, and that this love is there only because God himself is there.

Love has finally been explained and no argument from evil can ruin it. The God of the Christian Scriptures has explained love to us. And it is Jesus the Christ, the Son and God and second person of the Trinity who has demonstrated his love for humanity by giving his life on a Roman Cross for our redemption.

21. Revelation 21:4.

7

Coping with the Truth

Love and the Christian God

EVERYTHING SAID THUS FAR may be summed up in the fact that apart from the Christian worldview there is very little philosophical or religious reflection that can satisfy the question of love's origin with a meaningful response. All other attempts to understand love have left it in murky obfuscation. Through that haze only one reasonable response has emerged, giving us an answer to love that corresponds most coherently with reality. In other words, we now have the truth.

Imagine a man living his entire life behind the walls of a prison. Having been born there, he remained there, restricted to a world of grey stone where the light of day, like a golden shadow from an unknown source, would rarely come to linger on the walls of his cell. Year after year, he would listen as other prisoners spoke of a world beyond the steel bars, but of this world he knew nothing. Such talk seemed strange to him, and so he lived each day in silent doubt of anything beyond his walls. Imagine that one day a voice spoke to him from the other side of a wall telling him that he could, if he so desired, open his door and leave at any time he wished since the doors of the prison had never been locked. This of course, seemed rather foolish to him; after all, he had never seen the door open before and had no reason to leave. And so he finished his days, never trying the door, never seeking the truth, and never knowing what lay beyond that place.

Knowing the truth, knowing that you know the truth, and even liking the truth, are three very different things. Truth has been and will be encountered, assumed or denied by every human being at some level, and this makes truth impossible to ignore. Even those who flat-out reject truth's existence assume certain truths about reality in order to live their lives. Truth can be wonderfully refreshing and even thoroughly liberating as it enlightens and engages us. However, truth can also be equally offensive and depressing. I suppose it all depends on which side of the truth one stands. Every human being will face the hard reality of mistakenness at some point in their lives. Some will intentionally purport falsity; some will unknowingly defend falsity; and all will be swayed by falsity at some time and to some degree. False beliefs may be held in spite of genuine interest in the truth, or they may be created for the purpose of deception. In the search for love's source, various truths and falsities make themselves available. The worldviews and philosophical outlooks we have explored vary in their ability to communicate truth about love's existence. Some are uninformed, some are off-key, and others do little more than bloviate excremental fumes. One position alone remains truthful among the rest and that is the Christian worldview.

A Christian might read all of this and feel rather pleased by the idea that he got it right. He might feel some pride in the fact that his worldview best accounts for love's existence. He might even feel the desire to mock the non-believer by pointing his finger at his fellow human's folly. He might do all of this with a new found sense of confidence in himself, but what he should realize, rather, is that the truth about love does not depend on him. The Christian is privileged to live with the wonderful truth about love but, still, this truth is not of his making. He has no right to scoff at anyone. This is an essential point, because what we choose to do with Christianity, based upon its explanation for love, is a matter of humility and intellectual responsibility. The Christian is not the creator of truth, but is rather, the follower of truth's leading.

On the other hand, those who adhere to any worldview other than Christianity might find the evidence for the God of Christianity confused, rude, and unacceptable. Some might dare to believe it, many will scoff at it, and others will hate it, but again the truth about love does not depend on any amount of denial. If truth corresponds to reality then it is reasonable to assert that one is justified in believing it. Philosophical attempts to redefine reality and second-guess the basic contents of knowledge will, in no practical way, bypass the truth of the matter. We need not open bottomless pits of refutation and counter-refutation concerning theories of justification in epistemology to arrive at the acceptance of

Christianity as the most valid worldview for explaining love's existence. It is much more simple than this, really. All that is being suggested is that since Christianity best explains the origin and existence of love, it is reasonable to accept Christianity's explanation. Even when refused and declined adamantly, the reality behind the explanation still obtains.

Coping with this truth may be as difficult for the Christian as for the non-Christian in that the Christian will wonder why he is not leaps and bounds ahead of the non-Christian in his ability to love. Moreover, the non-Christian will quickly realize that he and his non-Christian friends are often times, not only *as* loving, but *more* loving than the Christian. We have all heard stories of Christian pastors or priests who treat others harshly, who commit theft, who lie, or who engage in adulterous affairs with vulnerable women in their congregations. At that same time, most of us can point to at least one non-religious person who shuns evil and lives in such great love for others that he is admired and respected by all who know him. Among the adherents of Islam, Hinduism, and Buddhism love makes itself evident. Having shown up in both the likely and unlikely places, love is not always partial to religious belief. Christians are not privileged in the experience of love, even if they are the ones who worship the God from whom love flows. God's love is extended to the world, as is his grace. This common grace allows all human beings to drink in this divine thing we call love. Such grace allows us each to participate in this heavenly gift. Whether one believes in God or not makes little difference to the reality that love is seen among us only by God's grace. One can enjoy a fruit even while he denies the tree from which it came. However, in denying the tree, he will ultimately lose out on its abundance. The fullness of eternal love is only known through Christ.

All human beings may delight in love during the brief duration of life upon this earth, but there is much more to love for those who know Christ. Though Christians do not have privileged access to love in this life, they do enjoy a degree of love unknown to anyone outside of Christ. The salvation that comes by faith will ultimately lead to a complete transformation of the heart and mind and will lead the Christian into the eternal presence of he who *is* love. In God's eternal presence the Christian will be perfected in love, and will experience love in all its unveiled glory.

THE LOVE OF GOD

Love is more than simple willed altruism; it is more than just goodwill; it is more than either kindness or concern for others by themselves; and it is certainly much more than yearning passion. But all of these together generate a definition, and on this definition one can elaborate by affixing such elements as mercy, forgiveness, and grace. More than a simple intellectual affirmation, love does not flow from God only as a rational pronouncement of his divine character; and more than a sentimental declaration, God's love is not reducible to a cuddly, giggling emotivism. If the Christian is to remain true to a biblical understanding of love then neither of these extremes will do. If God's love is divorced from its biblical reality we are left either with a love that is dry, stale, and cerebral or a love that is saturated with unthinking sentiment. If every example of God's love in Scripture is lifted from its context and pieced together to form a theology, this theology might resemble anything but the truth.

Such fatuous interpretations of God's love must be replaced with a love that exists in proper context to all of God's other attributes. God is not only love. He is good; he is holy; he is just; he is powerful, wise, and merciful. If a division is cleaved between his wisdom and his love, then we are left with a God who loves in an inane and undiscerning manner. If division is cleaved between his justice and his love, then we are left with a God who is our friend, but a God who cannot be our king.

God's love must not be reduced to simple willed altruism nor must it be reduced only to mere feeling. D.A. Carson has pointed out that two word groups are used in the New Testament for describing the love of God as seen in John 3:35 and 5:20, where it is said that God the Father loves God the Son. The first time this is said, the Greek text refers to love that is willed and self-sacrificial, but the second time, the text employs the terminology of friendship and emotional love.[1] The contrast is in the words *agapē* and *phileō*. Though both words are used to refer to God's love, each presents a form of love that is appropriate to the context. In a similar way, 1 Corinthians 13 demonstrates that love is more than willed altruism in that even those who engage in the most extreme acts of self-denial but do not have love are no more than a clattering gong or resounding cymbal.[2]

---

1. Carson, *Difficult Doctrine*, 26–27.
2. Ibid., 28.

God's passionate love is seen clearly in passages like Hosea 11 were God speaks of his desire to show mercy and kindness toward his people in spite of the fact that they have hated and betrayed him. Later, in the oft quoted text, John 3:16, we see clearly the goodness of God's love and his altruism in sending his Son, the Lord Jesus, to die in our place on the cross. It is said that God *so* loved the world that he gave his Son to die for it. This *gift of genuine benevolence and of merciful goodwill, passionately displayed, and emanating from an altruistic concern* is, as Carson points out, significant "not because it is extended to so big a thing as the world, but to so bad a thing; not to so many people, but to such wicked people."[3] God does not take delight in the death and destruction even of the wicked, but desires that all might be saved.[4] Abounding in love, he has painfully given himself for the benefit of those who hate him.

Imagine a wealthy estate owner who one day decides that it is time to distribute his wealth to an heir. With no children of his own he is grieved that he must divide his wealth among his distant relatives, servants, and friends. He thinks carefully about his situation, and decides that he will go to an orphanage and bring home a son who will someday inherit his entire estate.

He gathers his servants, readies his carriage, and sets out in search of a son. Past his gardens, his fields, and his stables, and on through the iron gate that separates his vast estate from the world, he rides to the nearest orphanage. He enters that place of the abandoned, and looks for a son among the many children that are presented to him. He interviews each one. He is looking for just the right child to make his own. He is looking for the one who will come into his home and be his son. One by one they are brought before him, but none of them will do.

On to the next orphanage he goes, again looking for a son. The second orphanage is the same as the first. Though the children are well behaved and polite they are not what he is looking for. He notices that in these orphanages each of these children is well taken care of and each has been given a proper education. In fact, each of these children is loved and each is nourished. "Have you any others," he asks. The keeper of the orphanage responds, "what else could you possibly want?" The man rises to leave, and tells his driver to take him to the worst orphanage he can find.

3. Ibid., 17.
4. Ezekiel 33:11; 1 Timothy 2:1–6.

They search for several days, and through the squalor of the poor districts they find a wretched miserable orphanage like none they have seen before. Through the filth and rubbish they walk, and come upon the front door. It is a drafty dilapidated door. They knock. The door falls from its hinges. They are met by the pungent stench of human excrement and disease. Gazing into the darkness and reek, the servant refuses to enter, and so the estate owner goes alone. The pestilential environment is like a wholly different world. He sees the ragged bodies of half-starved children lying about on the cold slate floor.

Through another door he walks and the image is worse. He goes to the head of the orphanage, a tired withered old man, and asks to see the very worst of the children; the most bitter, wretched, and miserable of them all. The old man curses under his breath and creeps away. After a moment he returns with the most pathetic creature the man has ever seen. The child is filthy and grimy and covered with sores. The estate owner stands there for a moment watching the boy. When finally their eyes meet, the child rushes on him spitting and kicking and flailing his arms.

"This one is full of spite and malice," the old man laughs.

"May I take him away from here?" asks the estate owner.

"For a price," demands the old man.

"How much?"

"Five years' wages."

"That seems high."

"Ten years' wages, and no less." The price was paid, and the boy was taken, kicking and screaming from the orphanage.

Now imagine, as unlikely as it would seem, that the old man had demanded the estate owner's life in exchange for the ragged malicious boy. Imagine that the estate owner had accepted such an offer. This is much like the love of God. Christianity has claimed that God has gone to the orphanage of earth and adopted as sons the loathsome and damned, and offered them a place of comfort in his presence. In consideration of the beauty of God's love in adopting the worst of humanity, the image above is an obvious example. When God demonstrated his love for us, he did so even while we hated him. This makes love all the more beautiful, for the despicable wretch did nothing to earn the grace given him, just as the slave did nothing to merit his adoption into glory.[5]

---

5. Galatians 4:3–7.

In the present age, we are told that if a person wants something he must simply reach out and take hold of it. A right decision, a shrewd manipulation, and an occasional despotic act can bring about the desired end. We call this ambition, but in the realm of spiritual things it may be better referred to as tyranny. The spiritual tyrant is he whose god accepts him on merit. The spiritual tyrant barters with his god to get his way. He make rules that require nothing of inner humility and true repentance, keeps them some of the time, and demands proper compensation. The spiritual tyrant religiously says and does all the right things and demands that others do the same, and in doing so deceives his god into delighting in this tyrant's holiness. His manipulative character is seen clearly when he lets on that his god has done something gracious when all the while it is the tyrant who has saved himself. Yet, this religious man has saved himself from nothing but humble contrition before a holy God. In fact, this spiritual tyrant has created a world in which God's grace and man's repentance are swept beneath a rug so that he may reach out and take hold of his own salvation. Such proud and optimistic claims on eternity are precisely that which Christianity opposes, for there is no ounce of tyranny in God's gracious love. Instead, we find a benevolent decree of love that saves us from our own tyrannical ways. God does not allow for the tyranny that comes when we love him first, for if he did, he would be obliged to allow us to exercise our say in how he must respond to our "great and worthy act." Rather, God loves us first and extends his perfect, good, and gracious love to us, driving away the constant fear of spiritual failure that naturally flows from self-reliance.

God's love is thus demonstrated in his grace—a grace that saves the cursed orphan in spite of his loathsome ways. Moreover, God's love is demonstrated in his forgiveness of the seemingly unforgivable. The anatomy of forgiveness is captured so beautifully when one considers the way in which some victims have pardoned the same odious scoundrels who abused them in the first place. The murderer, the thief, the rapist, and all the other sordid scalawags of this kind are those who take and give nothing in return. The forgiver, in contrast, does exactly the opposite. He gives so that more may be given in return. When God forgives man, he gives him perfect love, eternal life, and the occasion to give worship back to the giver.

God's forgiveness has been extended to those who have only taken so that even they might have something to give. God's love is the answer to the human condition—the condition that so clearly depicts an image of deposed royalty. We were offered life and love and eternity. We even tasted that good life and made a choice to discard it. The choice seemed good—a life of freedom and independence with no God as sovereign over us—but as Genesis 3 records, the choice brought the loss of an incorruptible moral status. We ushered in the dawn of a new world with all the horror of estrangement from God and the doom of depravity resulting in death. Pride became a blinder over our eyes, and we fell into destruction. The perfect God would not stand in the presence of imperfection. Each subsequent generation has endured the defect of sin that has led to our demise. "Flesh gives birth to flesh," said Christ.[6] The guilt of one man gives birth to the guilt of another, and so each carries with him the guilt of eternal death. We all have rebelled. The punishment is just: complete and eternal separation of humanity from the divine. This is what led to the dual nature of humanity. This is how greatness and wretchedness took form, and led to the forgiveness that God deemed good to lavish upon us in love.

Forgiveness came to us by means of thoughtful and assiduously unremitting love that was purposefully poured out upon us as Romans 5:5 makes clear. It is important in this text to note that God's love is *poured* and not simply dumped, dropped, or spilled. There is purpose and direction behind it that serves a specific end. It is never carelessly slopped upon us as one would slop waste, refuse, or other distasteful things into a pit. Just as a pure and savory wine is always directed with care into the appropriate piece of glassware, so is the sweet and nourishing love of God poured generously upon humanity. The forgiveness that flows to humanity from God's love is one of redemption and restoration. This reinstatement of man into relationship with his Creator is made all the more beautiful when one understands that though every human deserves to pass into the eternal night of abandonment, the King has gone to his death on behalf of the liar, the recalcitrant, the rebel, the murderer, and the scoundrel. In essence, the Son of God, Jesus Christ, has gone to the cross to die a death on our behalf, to appease the wrath of a holy God so that an unholy humanity might taste forgiveness. This is love.

There is a Swedish proverb that says that "love is like dew that falls on both nettles and lilies." From the Christian perspective this is true. God's good pleasure in loving us is not dependent on our moral beauty. Whether

6. John 3:6.

a man's character is likened to the grandeur of a rose or the repugnancy of a decaying carcass, God's favor and love might just as easily rest upon him. Whether he appears as a precious stone or a grimy alluvial deposit, it is by God's grace that love is extended to him. This gracious love is made all the more astounding when one realizes that there are neither roses or gems among us. The love that rains down upon this fallen humanity is better likened to dew that settles only upon the nettles.

A perfect God took the place of his imperfect Creation. A God of love took the place of his prideful, lustful, concupiscent, licentious, arrogant, deceitful, hateful, and recalcitrant creatures. The only God capable of love "demonstrated his own love for us in this: while we were still sinners, Christ died for us."[7] If love exists, then that love flows from a God who is by his nature loving. Furthermore, if that love is true and real, then it can be known. Real love comes unto humanity by the grace of a real God.

Consider one more analogy that may help clarify the immensity of God's grace and the perfection of his holiness. Imagine an artist who has poured his talent into creating a painting so splendid and magnificent that the world will never again see its equal. For years he toils to achieve the perfect ratios of color and light. Each line and curve and edge are meticulously placed. Complexity and simplicity come together in flawless harmony and the beauty of the image is mesmerizing to all. The work so greatly captures the artist's brilliance, and so greatly evokes emotion in its viewers that anyone who looks upon it is immediately delighted. When the work is finished the artist hangs it in a special room that he has built in his house for this one purpose. He keeps the door locked when he is away and tells his young son never to enter the room alone. His masterpiece is far too precious and must not be carelessly handled.

There the painting remains for some time until one day the boy finds the key and enters the room alone. He looks around the sees his father's painting tools: palates and paints, brushes and knives, oil, turpentine, and all the other things necessary to an artist. In curiosity and defiance he begins to open the paints and mix them on the palate. He is delighted by the affects of the turpentine and other chemicals as he pours them on the paint. But this game soon loses its appeal. Just then, he glances up and sees his father's masterpiece in the corner of the room. He takes the chemical and splashes a small amount on the bottom cor-

7. Romans 5:8.

ner of the canvas. He watches as the paint boils and dissolves before him in a mélange of color. He continues again and again to soak the painting until the diluted paint runs down upon the floor. By the time his fun is over there is nothing left of the masterpiece. It is ruined completely. Realizing the travesty of what he has done, the boy quickly leaves the room, locking the door behind him and carefully putting the key back in its place.[8]

This utterly stupid thing that the boy has done cannot be undone. No price can be put on that which is priceless. No amount of talent on the boy's part can fix this mess. He can never even begin to satisfy the debt that he has created for himself. Only one man can recreate that which has been destroyed, and that man is the artist himself. No one but the artist himself can satisfy the liability that now exists.

In the same way, the price of human rebellion against God cannot be satisfied by humanity. A perfectly holy God cannot be satisfied by anything less than a perfectly holy God, and a perfectly loving God can give nothing less than himself for a failed people. The cross of Christ is the only possible retribution for the debt of a defaced and ruined relationship. God's love is such that he himself has restored what we have ruined.

Humans will only ever know love by knowing God the Father because God himself is love. They will only ever know God the Father by knowing God the Son because he is the only bridge across the abyss of death. The significance of divine love is not found in the human desire to love God, but in God's love for human beings. This love is not dependent on humans as is the love of other gods. The triune God of Christianity is the only God capable of love in complete independence from his Creation, because each person of the Trinity loves the others in complete unified communion. C. S. Lewis has said:

> In God there is no hunger that needs to be filled, only plenteousness that desires to give. The doctrine that God was under no necessity to create is not a piece of dry scholastic speculation. It is essential . . . God, who needs nothing, loves into existence wholly superfluous creatures in order that he may love and perfect them.[9]

8. I am indebted here to Alexandre Sarran who provided the idea for this analogy in a sermon entitled, "Je Crois en Jésus-Christ," July 25, 2010.

9. Lewis, *Four Loves*, 126–27.

Love is not a human phenomenon. Love can come from no other place but from the inventor of love himself, the triune God, who is by his very nature loving. God cannot not love, and humans cannot love if not for God.

THE LOVE OF MAN

Having been knit together and formed by the hand of God, having received the breath of life, and having awakened for the first time to Creation, man was given God's image. Part of this divine gift was the moral awareness that illuminated to him the reality of love. Before his fall into spiritual ruin man could truly love God because the purity of his mind and spirit were intact. The only moral dilemma with which he was faced was the decision of whether or not to obey the only command given him. We have already discussed this choice and many of the implications thereof, and so there is no need to reiterate everything here. However, one of the significant effects of man's Fall into his present accursed state is the confusion and deterioration of love within his heart and mind. The significance of this reality was made clear when God demanded love as adoration. To love God was the highest and only way to reach a state of complete restoration and enjoy communion with God once more. As Matthew 22:34–40 tells us, the greatest commandment is love for God, and from this flows the second commandment, love for one's neighbor. The possibility of human redemption was built upon this: "love the Lord your God with all your heart and with all your soul and with all your mind . . . and love your neighbor as yourself.[10] Everything else hangs on this simple two-fold commandment.

We might better understand what it means to love both God and man if we examine individually each of the commandment's two parts. The first part sheds light on our love in relationship to God and his perfect love, the second part sheds light on our responsibility to our fellow man.

When we are commanded to love God, we are commanded to do so perfectly, with all our being. The perfection of our love is demanded because God's love is itself, perfect. It is this perfection that demonstrates again and again the shortcomings of man. If we are to ask whether there are varying degrees of perfection in love as there are varying degrees of intensity found in the light of the sun, the answer must be no, for

10. Matthew 22:37–39.

perfection itself would not be such if it could in some way be reduced. So it must be said with certainty that God's perfect love has made itself the standard by which all love is measured.

Who other can claim to be perfect in the same way that God is perfect? What man, what lesser being, can claim that he has attained all that is God? No one indeed can make such a claim! All things flow from God, and all things are distinctly different than he. The universe was not made from the substance of the perfect God, or from anything else for that matter. It was not made *from* anything; rather, it was made *by* someone. God does not create in the same way a painter or sculptor creates. What painter has said "let there be paint" and watched the paint appear before him? What sculptor has spoken a word to the darkness and watched as a lump of marble and chisel suddenly materialize from out of the non-existent?

God is distinctly other than man. He is distinctly other than his creation. God's creation does not share equal status with him. To equate God's creation with God himself is to entertain the tarnished thoughts in which pantheism festers. This is why it was necessary that the people of ancient Israel abstained from making images of God as commanded in the Decalogue, for to represent God by any created thing was to restrict and limit his glorious and otherworldly perfection. The perfection of God is evident in all of his attributes. He is perfect in holiness; he is perfect in justice; he is perfect in wisdom, in goodness, and in righteousness. He is ontologically, morally, and intellectually perfect. In the same way, his love is perfect. And if his love is perfect, then there is no time when God's love can fail.[11] Love's perfection implies love's consistency. This fact of love's perfection is essential to understanding Christ's commandment in Matthew 22, for even where the greatest love exists among humanity it is evident that there is little in human beings that emulates God's perfect love. One begins to wonder if perhaps Jesus has given us an impossible standard—a standard that can only be reached with God's help. To love God with all of one's heart, soul, and mind is to love him with all of one's being and to do so perfectly.

To be a perfect human means to love God perfectly. This was his original intent for man. However, man can fail at being man. In other words, man can fail at living up to the expectation intended for him, and ultimately fail at love. God, on the other hand, can never fail to be God.

11. 1 Corinthians 13:8.

He can never fail to be what he is. Who can rightly say that God has failed to be holy at times? Who can say that God has lost his omniscience if only for a moment? Who can say that God has ceased to love even the most miserable and wretched outcast upon this earth? These things cannot be, for God owns his attributes perfectly.

If God's holiness ceased for even a moment, what would be said, that God is only mostly holy? God's holiness can never cease, for God is by nature holy and this is proclaimed within the tenets of Christianity that have come from the Holy Scriptures themselves. He is holy to the utmost quality. This same criterion must apply to God's justice, goodness, righteousness, grace, mercy, omniscience, power, and wisdom. And certainly this principle must also apply to God's love. As said before, God *is* love. He is nothing shy, nothing exiguous, nothing sparse of this standard. With this standard of measurement, the purity of one's love may be understood by its relationship to God. All that God does is done through his right and holy love. Even his wrath against the ungodly is done in context to his love. Carson has said:

> God's wrath is not an implacable, blind rage. However emotional it may be, it is an entirely reasonable and willed response to offenses committed against his holiness. But his love . . . wells up amidst his perfections *and is not generated by the loveliness of the loved.* Thus there is nothing intrinsically impossible about wrath and love being directed toward the same individual or people at the same time. God in his perfections must be wrathful against his rebel image-bearers, for they have offended him; God in his perfections must be loving toward his rebel image-bearers, for he is that kind of God.[12]

Even amidst God's wrath, justice, and holiness, he is a God of perfect love.

Human love must be measured by the standard of God's perfection. If anyone ceases to love in any way and at any time then love no longer retains its perfection within that person. Love at this point is no longer a property that defines the human being. He may be defined as a human who has acted in love, but he may not be defined as one who is by nature loving. In fact, it is rare that humans retain any amount of love whatsoever. It is certain that man is made up of many things but love is not chief among them.

12. Carson, *Difficult Doctrine*, 69.

The greatest command of Christ is to love the Lord God with one's entire heart, soul, and mind. Not *some*, but *all*. In light of God's perfection and his demand for perfect love from his Creation, human beings have fallen so short of this standard that it is difficult to even recognize times when love is evident. Perhaps with great rarity man will demonstrate his love for God through some action of obedience, but this is done only briefly, of course, until he is distracted. We humans cannot love God consistently within our being. We cannot attain this perfection. We cannot close our eyes, clench our fists, direct the pained expression on our face to the sky and declare, "I love you, I love you, I love you, God!" What good does this do? It is clearly not enough.

In consideration of human failings, true love would seem to be elevated to the heavenly realm leaving humans to find love's imitations in friendships, in sensual eroticism, or in instinctual affections. Since we humans have failed so soundly at fulfilling the greatest command, we have thoroughly ostracized ourselves from communion with the divine. God does indeed demand an impossible standard. But the beauty of the whole rotten mess that man has made for himself is found precisely in the fact that God's standard is impossible for man. The only way to experience the love of God and to give one's love to God is by the grace of God. The Father God so *loved* the world that he gave his only Son, Jesus Christ, to take upon himself the wrath of God against the pride, the lust, the incorrigibility, and the sickness of evil and death in which humans wallow so that they might be saved if only they would repent and believe.

God's demand for perfect love proves two things. First, it proves that imperfect humans are incapable of God's standard of love apart from God himself. There is no possibility of human love apart from a divine source. Love is there only because God is there. Secondly, it proves that God must first extend his love to us if we are to respond in love and escape our doom. God's love seeks humans and finds them wherever they are. It pierces the dark places of the world and points always to the Trinity.

As a result of God's love for humans, he has allowed that some may be counted among those who love him, and by God's grace each of these is then able to love others. This brings us to the second part of Christ's commandment: Love your neighbor as yourself. This statement flows naturally from the first. In fact, the first is impossible without the second, since love for God is demonstrated by love for one's fellow man. Moreover, the second is impossible without the first, since love for God is the only real motivation for any other love whatsoever. The distinctive characteristics of God's love for the world are now turned horizontal as humans are called to love one another. It is because of God's love for his followers that his followers can likewise exhibit love for each other. In essence, this is one way in which the love of God is manifested among humans. When Christians love one another they are participating in the love of God. This important element of God's love must not be effaced or withdrawn from among Christians. If brotherly love is removed what is left but a cold dead empty vault. A vault is not a desirable thing, and if it can be helped, the Christian must not contribute needlessly to the inauguration of such a dismal reality by his failure to love his brother.

If we humans ever are to love well, where do we begin? It is clear that love is not something we are good at. It is not something that comes naturally to us. Consider the beginnings of a human life. A child's life begins in selfishness and coveting. Generosity, kindness, patience, sympathy, and compassion are not expected of him, nor is he capable of them. As an infant he is waited on like a little lord or nobleman, not necessarily because he is noble but because his survival depends on it. On a whim he calls for his meals or his bed. When unhappy, he requires someone to entertain him, and he lounges in a carriage while others are made to walk. He lives as king because there is no other way in which he can live. Only by years of training in maturity will he begin to overcome his tyrannical autocracy over others and live in a more tolerable relationship to other human beings. Sadly, it is rare that we humans move beyond infancy so that we might love in maturity.

By nature we are pinned beneath a litany of realities that obstruct our ability to love. To love is to struggle continually against our rotten nature. How then do we love? Is there a recipe or formula to follow? Do we simply mix for ourselves a concoction of willpower and good intentions and top it off with a dash of overall pleasantness? Do we write a daily list of loving actions that must be performed for others? I am not convinced that love could ever be attained in these ways.

Never will we love perfectly simply by resolving to do so. Resolve may produce the affects of love but it will not lend itself to changing the heart or the mind. One does not change one's mind. The mind is changed when it is illuminated to a grander or truer reality. In the same way, one does not easily change one's heart or emotional state. The heart is transformed when it is softened to the reality that it has been offered grace, and that by receiving grace it can in turn give grace. Many will live their lives by imitating love only because they have resolved to do so, but only some few will receive love and allow it to transform them.

It is only under the canopy of God's grace that we can ever hope to love. If we are to more fully love our neighbor, then we are to begin by more fully understanding the Gospel. If we are to grow in love, then we are to begin by absorbing the truth of God's grace that will transform us from objects of wrath to sons of glory. If we are to grow in our love for others, then we best begin by enjoying the sapid qualities of God's unfathomable love as it is revealed to us piece by piece. This love is that which lays siege upon unrepentant hearts until they are softened from hatred and ultimately redeemed. Those redeemed can then enjoy God's perfect love. Being loved, they become rich, and being rich they have plenty to give to others, for to love others one must first delight in God's gracious love.

GOD'S LOVE AS IT RELATES TO OUR ETERNITY

Before man's eternal destiny in light of God's love can be examined, several conclusions must initially be drawn from the combined previous discourse. Firstly, as has already been demonstrated, love exists. Though love eludes us frequently, and though we find its fruit more often tainted by the weeds of hatred, it has been seen. Secondly, this love can be explained by no other than the Christian God. This eternal and necessary God has given himself the name "I Am."[13] He is the one who *was*, and *is*, and *will be*.[14] His knowledge, power, and goodness cannot be restricted by anything either within or *sans* creation. Thirdly, God never fails to be God, nor does his love ever fail. There is no dark abysmal depth where one might escape from the light of God's love. This inescapable and unfailing love stands in great contrast to the fallibility of the corporeal world of which humans are a part. Under the curse of sin all that is material has been subjected to frailty in the same way that the mind has fallen into decay. The human being will fail, spoil, or deteriorate. His corrupted body will end in death and his corrupted spirit will face its Maker.

13. Exodus 3:14.
14. Revelation 1:4, 8.

I emphasize this third point because it is vital to how love affects the life to come. For the Christian there are only two ways in which God's love will be experienced by those who slowly expire from this present life. We will either enjoy it eternally or suffer without it.

Unlike God, each human being will fail to retain the characteristics that help define them. In fact, it is like this with most things we experience in this life. Shadows shift; light is created and absorbed; things move, sway, and collide and life comes and goes. That which grows, will change, and then will die. Take a tree, for example. If I were to describe a typical leaf bearing tree, I would say the tree was tall (at least taller than I). If I were to look at it in the summer months, I would say that it is green. I would say that its trunk is cylindrical, and its limbs protrude from it like a purely nature excrescence from its trunk. I would say that its roots extend down into the soil to draw out moisture and nutrients. I might even describe the process of photosynthesis, and on I could go.

However, what if such a magnificent tree were to fail at all of those things that constitute its treeness? In other words, what if the tree were to be stripped of its leaves? Certainly we may still call it a tree since we can still ascertain the tree-like characteristics it retains. But what if it were to be stripped of its branches and shape and color? What if it were to be deprived of its magnificence and splendor? What if its roots were cut away and its bark peeled from it like paint from a wall? Would such a mutilated and malformed thing—a botanical misfit—still be considered a tree? Hardly! It might be called a post or a stump, but certainly not a tree. The tree would lose its identity, its integrity, and its distinctiveness. This prosaic and altogether ordinary lump would thus fail at all of those things that make it a tree. At some point in time every tree will fail to be a tree. At some point in time every created thing will fail to bear those marks that define it. Deterioration sets in.

This, I suppose, is no more than a fancy way of saying that we all must die. But in the meantime, God will go on loving us. There is no earthly escape. Being unable to escape from love in this life, humans will then have to make a decision as to whether or not they will choose to escape from love in the next. The joys of Heaven are experienced in the light of God's glory and the radiance of his love, but these joys have been reserved for those who accept them. Some have not. Some have hardened their hearts and cursed the God who so loved them. However, both must face him someday. In fact, Jesus himself said that there will come a day when those who humbly repent will be brought into the wedding banquet of Heaven, and those who have rejected him will be left out in the darkness with the doors forever locked.[15] Such language denotes banishment from the palace and confinement to the cold and dark night.

This banishment has been called Hell. It is a place—first and foremost—of separation from God. And with separation from God, Hell must also be a place of separation from love. C. S. Lewis has noted that "the only place outside Heaven where you can be perfectly safe from all the dangers and perturbations of love is Hell."[16] Lewis has implied that while Heaven means to be noticed by God, Hell means to be "absolutely outside—repelled, exiled, estranged, finally and unspeakably ignored."[17] To be ignored by God must be a dreadful thing, but it is not possible for any to experience such neglect in this life. Even for those who suffer greatly and harbor anger against God under the pretext that they have been abandoned, know nothing of real desertion. To be ignored will be reserved for the day when the doors of Heaven are shut against those who do not call upon the name of the Lord. On that day they will hear the dreaded words: "Away from me, I never knew you."[18] These words of exile decry each wretched soul to its doom, and separate eternally the created being from the Creator. The door to Heaven is closed and the lock set in place. Expulsion from God's presence, and ultimately God's love, becomes the reality of Hell.

But, can love be so easily escaped? Does Hell offer a true departure from God's love? Does God still peer into Hell as through tinted glass, seeing in, though those in Hell cannot see out? Is it possible that God could still love even those who chose eternal separation from him? Could it be that the one in Hell is doomed to fester in the wickedness of his own contriving without the slightest spirit of repentance and without the slightest knowledge of love? Could it be that he is doomed to look into the tinted glass and see only his wretched reflection, while God looks in and sees him clearly?

15. Matthew 22:1–14.

16. Lewis, *Four Loves*, 121.

17. Lewis, *Weight of Glory*, 41.

18. Matthew 7:23.

If Hell is a choice that humans crave, then it is not simply a place where God ignores man, but where man ignores God. Perhaps part of the suffering of Hell is in the human inability to respond to God's love. Perhaps part of the suffering of Hell is to know that God is there loving the damned of humanity and yet, these damned are unable and unwilling to love him back. Perhaps the one who resides there is doomed to an eternity of hating God in spite of God's love for him. Will he be ignored by God? Whether yes or no, it is certain that Hell is a place where love goes unrealized and unfulfilled. In Hell, love will be unknown to man. In Hell, he will be given over to his desire for absolute evil and the possibility of love will be extinguished.

The distinctiveness of Heaven, on the other hand, is in the overwhelming and permeating enjoyment of love that will forever delight those who stand in the presence of God. Unencumbered by sin and death, all the riches of God's glorious and inexhaustible love will be revealed to the once disgusting and pitiful beings who are now redeemed by grace. These redeemed and glorified ones will, for the first time, be enabled to love God perfectly. They will awaken to a day without end in the realm of the King where no lesser thing vies for the worship that is due the one and true Trinity. In this great realm the memory of hatred will fade like shadows in the morning light and God will be the only object of love.

I cannot help but imagine that place, and in doing so, realize that all the pithy things that occupy my time and demand my affection are displaced in the wake of love's abundance. If I am in any way deserving of love it is because God has made me so by his own good pleasure. If I am in any way able to love it is because God has permitted it and nurtured it within me. And if I am to give myself to love, then I must first give myself to God. The beginning of true love is in the knowledge that love must be directed toward the right object. By recognizing that right object as the God of the universe, love may be realized more readily and the *gift of genuine benevolence and of merciful goodwill, passionately displayed, and emanating from an altruistic concern* may then be given to others. For those who gratefully accept the grace of God in faith, the fullness of love will begin to blossom before them. For those living in God's love we have begun to taste the delightfulness of that pure and good thing. And one day, in Heaven, all the mysteries of love will be revealed and he who enters into that blessed realm will stand face to face with the inextinguishable love of God and weep no more.

LEAVING DIRT PLACE

God's love has not failed, not now, not ever. It is there because he is there. Only through him is love possible. I see it now as never before. For the first time it is made clear. I can finally love and know for certain the one from whom this love derives. I can live in confidence that love is far more than a philosophical theme to be explored or a vague concept to be made clear. True love is living. It is wholly real. If love is to be meaningful, if love is to be true, if love is to be personal, if love is to be active, if love is to be absolute, if love is to be knowable, then it must come from God. If love is to be love at all then it must come from the Trinity.

Love is not so frail as I once thought. The arid landscape of *Dirt Place* will be left behind. I had seen before the vacillating fragility of the human affections, but now I see that it is divine love alone that can bring meaning to these affections. It is divine love alone that substantiates these affections. It is divine love alone that has crept in to save us even when all our strength was given to resistance. It is finally made clear. I have not seen love anywhere apart from the Trinity. Any love that is, is of him and for him. By God's grace we humans meagerly attempt to imitate divine love and in doing so grow in this practice. We humans try our best to act in love at times, and we imitate the motions of love as a child imitates his father. But when we succeed it is by his divine purpose and pleasure. As an infant sees the grace of motion in his mother's steps, we crawl along as if walking were out of reach. But as we draw near to God, love becomes more real. We begin to walk. We begin to see.

In considering again all the worldviews and philosophical outlooks examined thus far, I will admit that love is possible even in the hearts of those who shake their fists at God. Yes, love can be shown by men who have no direct knowledge of him and no longing for him. Yes, love can be where the materialist is, and where the pantheist is, and where the polytheist is. Yes, love is possible for all, but it is the God of Christianity alone who is the one and only true source. It is this one and only true God from which all love ultimately flows. To be loved by him and to love him in return is the only final and lasting joy we will ever know. So, in repentance let us put off our frail affections and love him truly. Let us leave behind our inadequate philosophies and religions. Let us find contentment in the joy of his salvation; let us find delight in *Leaving Dirt Place*; and let us bask in the Trinity's everlasting love.

Bibliography

Abe, Masao. *Zen and Western Thought*. New York: Macmillan, 1985.

St. Augustine. *The Confessions*. Translated by Henry Chadwick. 1991. New York: Oxford University Press, 1998.

Beckwith, Francis J. "Moral Law, the Mormon Universe, and the Nature of the Right We Ought to Choose." In *The New Mormon Challenge: Responding to the Latest Defense of a Fast Growing Movement*. Edited by Fransic J. Beckwith, Carl Mosser, and Paul Owen. 219–242. Grand Rapids, Michigan: Zondervan, 2002.

Beilby, James K., Paul R. Eddy. *Divine Foreknowledge*. Downers Grove, Illinois: Intervarsity, 2001.

Berkowitz, Peter. *Nietzsche: The Ethics of an Immoralist*. Cambridge, Massachusetts: Harvard University Press, 1995.

Carson, D.A. *The Difficult Doctrine of the Love of God*. Wheaton, Illinois: Crossway, 2000.

Compte-Sponville, André. *L'Esprit de l'Athéisme: Introduction à une Spiritualité sans Dieu*. Paris: Editions Albin Michel, 2006.

Copleston, Frederick. *A History of Philosophy: Volume 7, Fichte to Nietzsche*. Mahwah, New Jersey: Paulist, 1963.

Corduan, Winfried. *Neighboring Faiths*. Downers Grove, Illinois: Intervarsity, 1998.

Cragg, Kenneth. *The Call of the Minaret*. New York: Oxford University Press, 1956.

Dawkins, Richard. "Atheists for Jesus." In *The Portable Atheist*. Edited by Christopher Hitchens, 307–310. Philadelphia: Da Capa, 2007.

———. *The Selfish Gene*, 30th Anniversary Edition. Oxford, England: Oxford University Press, 2006.

Demarest, Bruce A., Gordon R. Lewis. *Integrative Theology: Three Volumes in One*. Vol. 1. Grand Rapids, Michigan: Zondervan, 1996.

Dembski, William A. *The End of Christianity: Finding a Good God in an Evil World*. Nashville: B&H, 2009.

Dhavamony, Mariasusai. *Love of God According to Saiva Siddhanta: A Study in the Mysticism and Theology of Saivism*. Oxford: Oxford University Press, 1971.

Dickens, Charles. *A Tale of Two Cites*. Unabridged Charles Dickens. Philadelphia: Running, 1999.

Dostoevsky, Fyodor. *The Brothers Karamazov*. Translated by Constance Garnett. 1912. New York: Barnes and Noble, 2004.

Erickson, Millard J. *Introducing Christian Doctrine*. Grand Rapids, Michigan: Baker, 1992.

Geisler, Norman L., Abdul Saleeb. *Answering Islam: The Crescent in Light of the Cross*. 2nd Edition. Grand Rapids, Michigan: Baker, 2002.

Hallie, Philip P. *Lest Innocent Blood be Shed: The Story of the Village of Le Chambon and How Goodness Happened There*. New York: Harper & Row, 1979.

Harris, Sam. *Letter to a Christian Nation*. New York: Alfred A. Knopf, 2006.

Harrison, Paul. *The Elements of Pantheism: Understanding the Divinity in Nature and the Universe*. Boston: Element, 1999.

Hobbes, Thomas. *Leviathan*. Vol. 1. Chicago: Henry Regnery, 1956.

Holmes, Arthur F. *Fact, Value and God*. Grand Rapids, Michigan: William B. Eerdmans, 1997.

Hume, David. *Dialogues Concerning Natural Religion*. Edited Richard Popkin. Indianapolis: Hackett, 1980.

Hunt, John. *Pantheism and Christianity*. New York: Kennikat, 1970.

Jeffery, Arthur. *Islam: Muhammad and His Religion*. New York: Bobbs-Merrill, 1958.

Kant, Immanuel. *Grounding for the Metaphysics of Morals*. Translated by James Ellington. 1983. 2nd ed. Indianapolis: Hackett, 1994.

Keller, Timothy. *The Reason for God: Belief in an Age of Skepticism*. New York: Riverhead, 2008.

Kierkegaard, Søren. *Provocations: Spiritual Writings of Kierkegaard*. Edited and compiled by Charles E. Moore. Maryknoll, New York: Orbis, 2003

Kretzmann, P.E. *The God of the Bible and Other "Gods."* St. Louis, Missouri: Concordia, 1943.

Lewis, C. S. *The Abolition of Man*. New York: Harper Collins, 2001.

———. *The Four Loves*. New York: Harcourt, 1988.

———. *The Problem of Pain*. New York: Harper Collins, 2001.

———. *The Weight of Glory*. New York: Harper Collins, 2001.

Lubac, Henri de. *Aspects of Buddhism*. Translated by George Lamb. 1954. New York: Sheed and Ward, 1954.

May, Simon. *Nietzsche's Ethics and His War on Morality*. Oxford, England: Clarendon, 1999.

Merrien, Cathrine. *L'Amour*. Paris: Eyrolles, 2010.

Miller, David L. *The New Polytheism: Rebirth of the Gods and Goddesses*. New York: Harper & Row, 1974.

Miller, Elliot. "The Yoga Boom: A Call for Christian Discernment." Christian Research Journal, vol. 31, no. 2 (2008) 11–21.

Morris, Thomas V. *Making Sense of It All: Pascal and the Meaning of Life*. Grand Rapids, Michigan: William B. Eerdmans, 1992.

Myers, Sondra, and Carol Rittner. *The Courage to Care*. New York: New York University Press, 1986.

Nehls, Gerhard. *Christians Ask Muslims*. Bellville: SIM International Life Challenge, 1987.

Nietzsche, Friedrich. "Mixed Opinions and Maxims." In *The Portable Nietzsche*. Edited and translated by Walter Kaufmann, 64–67. 1954. New York: Viking Penguin, 1982.

———. "The Gay Science." In *The Portable Nietzsche*. Translated and edited by Walter Kaufmann, 93–101. 1954. New York: Viking Penguin, 1982.

———. "Beyond Good and Evil." In *Moral Philosophy: A Reader*, edited by Louis P. Pojman, 116–123. 3rd ed. Indianapolis: Hackett, 2003.

Parrish, Stephen E. "A Tale of Two Theisms: The Philosophical Usefulness of the Classical Christian and Mormon Concepts of God." In *The New Mormon Challenge: Responding to the Latest Defense of a Fast Growing Movement*. Edited by Fransic

J. Beckwith, Carl Mosser, and Paul Owen. 193–218. Grand Rapids, Michigan: Zondervan, 2002.

Pascal, Blaise. *Pensées.* 2nd edition. Translated by A.J. Krailsheimer. 1966. London: Penguin, 1995.

Penelhum, Terence. *Butler.* London: Routledge and Kegan Paul, 1985.

Peters, F. E. "The Origins of Islamic Platonism: The School Tradition." In *Islamic Philosophical Theology.* Edited by Parviz Morewedge. 14–45. Albany, New York: State University of New York Press, 1979.

Pink, Arthur W. *The Attributes of God.* Grand Rapids, Michigan: Baker, 1975.

Plantinga, Alvin. "Supralapsarianism, or 'O Felix Culpa.'" In *Christian Faith and the Problem of Evil.* Edited by Peter van Inwagen. 1–25. Grand Rapids, Michigan: William B. Eerdmans, 2004.

Rachels, James. *The Elements of Moral Philosophy.* New York: Random House, 1986.

Rahman, Fazlur. *Major Themes of the Qur'an.* Chicago: Bibliotheca Islamica, 1980.

Rand, Ayn. "A Defense of Ethical Egoism." In *Moral Philosophy: A Reader,* edited by Louis P. Pojman, 72–78. 3rd ed. Indianapolis: Hackett, 2003.

Russell, Bertrand. *A Free Man's Worship.* In *Moral Philosophy: A Reader,* edited by Louis P. Pojman, 313–317. 3rd ed. Indianapolis: Hackett, 2003.

Sagan, Carl. *Cosmos.* New York: Random House, 1980.

Sartre, Jean-Paul. *Existentialism and Human Emotions.* New York: Citadel, 1987.

Schaeffer, Francis. *He is There and He is Not Silent.* Wheaton, Illinois: Tyndale, 1972.

Schiffman, Richard. *Sri Ramakrishna: A Prophet for a New Age.* New York: Paragon, 1989.

Shakespeare, William. *Hamlet.* Oxford, England: Oxford University Press, 1987.

Sire, James W. *The Universe Next Door.* 5th ed. Downers Grove, Illinois: InterVarsity, 2009.

Smith, Joseph. *Teachings of Joseph Smith.* Compiled and edited by Joseph Fielding Smith. Salt Lake City: Deseret, 1976.

Stump, Eleonore. "The Mirror of Evil." In *God and the Philosophers: The Reconciliation of Faith and Reason,* edited by Thomas V. Morris, 235–247. New York: Oxford University Press, 1994.

Suzuki, Daisetz Teitaro. *What is Zen?* New York: Perennial Library, Harper & Row, 1971.

Torrey, Norman L. *Les Philosophes : The Philosophers of the Enlightenment and Modern Democracy.* New York: Capricorn, 1960.

Van Voorst, Robert E. *Anthology of World Scriptures. Rig-Veda* 10.129; *Brihad-Aranyaka Upanishad* 1.4.1–7. Belmont, California: Thomson Wadsworth, 2006.

Vroom, Hendrik M. *No Other Gods: Christian Belief in Dialogue with Buddhism, Hinduism, and Islam.* Grand Rapids, Michigan: William B. Eerdmans, 1996.

Watts, Alan. *The Way of Zen.* New York: Pantheon, 1957.

Wright, Robert. *The Moral Animal: Why We Are the Way We Are: The New Science of Evolutionary Psychology.* New York: Pantheon, 1994.